WELCOME TO CRAFT BEER

THE 365 BEST BEERS IN THE WORLD

Over the past decade, beer has changed forever. Gone are the days when craft beer was a fad, a niche activity enjoyed by the few and comparatively inaccessible for many who sought it out. Nowadays, craft beer is a truly global phenomenon that can be experienced almost anywhere in the world, from the United States to Japan to New Zealand and almost anywhere in between.

Over the next few pages, you'll find a collection of beers that we've arrogantly called 'the best beers in the world' and all of them are stunners. 'Best' is completely subjective of course, and you'll have to try them for yourself to see if you agree. Some you will be able to pick up right on your doorstep, and others may take considerable effort to find if you ever hope to try them. Regardless, we hope this collection of beers sends you on an exciting journey into the heart of our favourite fermented beverage.

Cheers!

"365 OF THE WORLD'S BEST BEERS TO ENJOY ALL YEAR ROUND, WHATEVER THE WEATHER"

FEATURES

365 BEST BEERS

MEET THE EXPERTS

Matthew Curtis is an award-winning freelance beer writer and UK editor for beer website and podcast, Good Beer Hunting. He sits on the board of the British Guild of Beer Writers and also writes for *Ferment Magazine, Belgian Beer and Food* and on his blog, Total Ales.
Twitter/Instagram: @totalcurtis
Web: www.goodbeerhunting.com

Chris Hall has been writing about beer since 2010, and is co-author of the previous issues of *Craft Beer* (Volume 1 of *365 Best Beers in The World* and *100 Best Breweries in The World*). Chris is also Media & Events Manager for London's Brew By Numbers.
Twitter/Instagram: @chrishallbeer
Web: www.chrishallbeer.com

Claire M. Bullen got her start working in beer six years ago, when she led craft beer walking tours in Brooklyn, New York. Now London-based, Claire has contributed writing to *Total Ales*, the *Evening Brews*, and writes a bi-monthly food and beer pairing column for *Hop Burns & Black*. She is a Cicerone® Certified Beer Server.
Twitter/Instagram: @clairembullen

UNDERSTANDING BEER STYLES

Beer has a huge variety of colours, flavours and origins, so how do you know what you're drinking? Here's our guide to the most common styles

Like gravity, beer styles had certainly existed for a long time, but weren't fully understood. The origins, stories, and connections between them all were mysteries, and it required a journalist with a nose for a story to get to the bottom of it all.

This beer equivalent of Isaac Newton, who documented and set out what the world's beer styles were, was a Yorkshireman by the name of Michael Jackson (1942-2007). Jackson was fascinated by the stories, the people, and the near-magical uniqueness of every beer he tasted, and he travelled the world trying to understand them all. His books, including *The World Guide to Beer* (1977), *Great Beers of Belgium* (1991) and *Beer Companion* (1993), were not just influential, but at least partially responsible for a global renaissance in beer appreciation. Craft beer is now a global, interconnected culture, and to make beers in styles from other countries, brewers can adjust recipes, use unusual equipment and even replicate the local water profile to help them do so.

As well as helping drinkers make sense of the beer they were drinking, Jackson helped brewers to better articulate their intentions. That's the main thing to understand about beer styles: it's a shorthand for what the brewer intended the beer to be. On the right you'll find a quick glossary covering many of styles you'll find in this guide: as 'esters', like banana, bubblegum, cloves and apples, all of which are most obviously present in unfiltered wheat beers.

"JACKSON WAS FASCINATED BY THE STORIES, THE PEOPLE, AND THE UNIQUENESS OF EVERY BEER"

style	description
Ale	A broad umbrella category for beers that undergo a warm fermentation. IPAs, Saisons, Stouts and Gueuze, for example, are all ales.
Double IPA	A stronger, more intense IPA, typically over 8% and with scaled-up hop additions to match.
Dubbel	A Belgian style of rich, brown ale with pronounced fruit notes from the yeast.
Gose	A German-style sour wheat beer that typically uses salt and coriander. Modern versions may add other ingredients such as fruit or spices.
Geuze/Gueuze	A sour beer made by blending different ages of lambic beers together.
Hefeweizen	A cloudy, German style of wheat beer with notes of banana and clove.
Helles	A light style of lager from Munich. Generally less hoppy than Pilsner.
Imperial Stout	Higher strength dark beers brewed for export and ageing. Once the preserve of the upper classes, now a favourite with beer geeks for their intensity.
India Pale Ale (IPA)	Normally a stronger Pale Ale, historically highly-hopped for preservation reasons (English/Traditional); but now highly-hopped for aroma and flavour (American).
Lambic	A spontaneously fermented beer from the Pajottenland region of Belgium, generally aged and blended to make styles such as geuze/gueuze (a blend of aged and young lambic refermented), sweetened faro, kriek (cherry beer) and framboise (raspberry beer).
Pale Ale	British examples (also called Bitter) are malty, bitter and herbal. American versions are typically stronger, with pronounced hop character. Belgian Pale Ales are dry, bitter and yeast-forward.
Pilsner	A pale golden lager with bitter hop character, originating in Pilsen.
Porter	Historically, a dark brown, oak-aged beer. Modern versions are frequently indistinguishable from Stout.
Quadrupel	A strong, dark Belgian abbey-style ale, often as strong as 10-12%.
Stout	A dark, rich ale. Historically, the stronger version of Porter, but now the terms are seen as being almost interchangeable.
Saison	A farmhouse ale originating in modern-day Belgium and France. A dry, bitter beer with pronounced yeast and spice notes.
Tripel	A strong, pale Belgian abbey style ale with fruity, spicy flavours.
Wild Ale	A catch-all term for farmhouse-style beers that use wild yeast strains, and potentially bacteria, barrels, fruit and other ingredients.
Witbier	A Belgian style of wheat beer, lighter in colour and flavour than German wheat beers, often using fruit peel and coriander seed.

COFFEE & BEER

Craft breweries are increasingly incorporating coffee in their beers in a variety of intriguing and delicious ways

Anyone who works in a brewery will tell you that it takes a lot of good coffee to make good beer. Brewers work early hours and have a taste for the finer things, including their coffee. In fact, a lot of brewery employees have some kind of background in coffee, and it sometimes feels like coffee geeks and beer geeks are basically the same set of people, and it just depends what time of day you catch them at. It was always just a matter of time until the two drinks became one.

Brewed coffee and beer have quite a lot in common: there are hundreds of ways to make it, the principal ingredients have characteristics based on where they are grown, both grain and coffee beans are roasted, water profile can make all the difference, and both are all about managing temperatures and extracting flavours.

That said, the use of coffee in beer is not an old tradition, born from the homebrewing community of the 1990s, and some beers with roast grains can have mild coffee flavours anyway. So why bother? Well, brewers have used fruit, spices, flowers and other natural ingredients for as long as beer has existed, and coffee is the latest of these to be used to add new dimensions of flavour.

Speciality coffee culture in the past 20 years has opened people's eyes to a huge variety of flavours, brew methods and coffees from around the world. Everything from tangerine, liquorice, blueberry, vanilla and coriander to delicate floral notes of jasmine can be found in coffee, in varieties diverse enough to rival hops.

Whilst most commonly used in dark beers, coffee is now used in everything from IPAs, saisons and sour beers to add unique new depths to our favourite beer styles. There are now even beer festivals dedicated to beers using coffee, so there's never been a better time to be a lover of these two truly global drinks.

HOW COFFEE CAN BE USED IN THE BREWING PROCESS

Brewers choose to add coffee in a variety of ways, depending on the beer they are making and the brewing equipment they have. Broadly, it comes down to whether it is added hot (usually before or during fermentation) or cold (after fermentation), and whether the coffee has been brewed, ground or added as whole beans.

HOT

Coffee added at high temperatures or as hot brewed coffee typically has more roast character and is more acidic, so is sometimes best suited to beers with lower roast notes and acidity.

COLD

Coffee added at cold temperatures or as cold brew will add less bitterness and acidity, is often best employed in beers that already have pronounced roast notes and bitterness.

GROUND COFFEE

If ground, coffee will release its aromatics and flavours more quickly and intensely, but these can fade quickly, so freshness is key.

WHOLEBEAN COFFEE

If the coffee isn't ground, it will release its flavours more slowly, which is useful if you want to finely control and monitor the intensity of coffee notes added.

AGEING BEER: WHAT TO DRINK AND WHAT TO SAVE

Most beer is best enjoyed fresh, but here's a quick guide on how to get the most out of the beers in your collection that will appreciate with time

Although the majority of beer is best enjoyed fresh, there are many that will benefit from carefully considered ageing. Successfully doing so will mean that you can enjoy the transformation of flavours over a great deal of time. Before you head out to your nearest bottle shop to stock up however, you'll need to make sure you've got a suitable space in which to store your beers. Not everyone will have his or her own cellar but wherever you do store your beer you need to ensure that it is cool, free of sunlight and keeps a consistent temperature. Your 'cellar' will need to be free of UV light and spikes in temperature that could cause unwanted off flavours to form in your beer.

With your space set up it's time to buy some beer – you'll just have to temper your enthusiasm so you don't drink your collection before it's had a proper chance to develop. When it comes to ageing beer, your best friend is alcohol – as a general rule higher alcohol beers will age better than low alcohol ones, with the booze being far more sympathetic to the development of any off flavours. It also means that when the beer begins to oxidise, and it will go through many peaks and troughs as it does, the alcohol will be there too support it. If it pays off the result will be delightful notes of boozy stone fruit, not unlike a port or sherry. Imperial stouts, doppelbocks and barley wines are your friends here.

Not everything in a high ABV beer will survive though – so sometimes it's not always best to rely on alcohol to preserve the flavours you want to enjoy. Beers that use highly volatile ingredients such as coffee or those that are dry hopped will loose those flavours just as quickly as if it were a pale ale. As an example, Founders Kentucky Breakfast Stout will develop beautifully over time, but if you really enjoy its coffee profile then there is little to no point in letting it age.

Some of the most satisfying beers to age are sours, farmhouse ales or anything fermented with 'wild' yeast strains such as Brettanomyces. The first advantage of this is that usually a small portion of live yeast will remain in the bottle and continue to eat up any residual sugars, as well as any pesky oxygen, as long as it remains alive. This makes Belgian lambic and gueuze perfect to age, despite the ABV being relatively low – although anything similar from elsewhere in the world will appreciate over time just as well.

Of course the most important thing when it comes to ageing beer is having more than one bottle in your collection so that you can observe directly how it changes over time. The Trappist beer Orval is perfect for this – a case is relatively good value and with live Brettanomyces in the bottle you can observe how it gradually transforms from a bright, hoppy Belgian pale into a far more funky, complex and curious beer. Just try not to drink it all at once.

"WHEN IT COMES TO AGEING BEER, YOUR BEST FRIEND IS ALCOHOL"

THE BATTLE OF THE IPAS: EAST COAST VS WEST COAST

After decades of West Coast dominance, the East Coast IPA is making a splash. What's next for this latest evolution in the American IPA?

In the American brewing scene, the differences between the West Coast IPA and the East Coast – or New England-style – IPA – are providing a glimpse into the way this style is changing, evolving and even splintering.

Few beers have captured the public imagination quite like the IPA. Distinctly different from the maltier, lower-alcohol, less intensely hopped British IPA, the American IPA first found its footing on the West Coast. Some point to the release of Anchor Liberty Ale – technically a pale ale, but made with Cascade hops – in 1975 as the very beginning of the style.

In the ensuing years, many of the earliest and most influential American craft breweries set up shop on the West Coast, and began experimenting with hop-driven brewing, particularly with American-grown hops that were, as a rule, powerful in their bitterness but also much richer in juicy, tropical fruit, and citrus flavours than their European counterparts. Sierra Nevada was launched in Chico, California in 1979, and soon made waves with its Pale Ale, which was the hoppiest beer around at its time of release. In 1994, Blind Pig, now defunct but formerly based in Temecula, California, turned out an Inaugural Ale that went even heavier on the hops, and is now considered the first-ever double IPA.

From these early innovators followed a wave of West Coast breweries that made their names with hoppy IPAs. Stone Brewing launched in Escondido, California in 1996, with a range of hop-driven styles; Green Flash began brewing in San Diego in 2002, and their West Coast IPA helped codify the burgeoning style; Russian River's Pliny the Younger, a potent and hugely in-demand triple IPA, has been brewed since 2005.

With each passing year, demand for and interest in the West Coast IPA grew. 2010 is cited as the high water mark of the style: the year drinkers couldn't get enough of that bracing bitterness; those distinctive flavours of grapefruit, pine, resin and citrus; that caramel malt base; and those intensely high ABVs and IBUs.

But with every trend follows a backlash. That might explain the success of the East Coast-style IPA today, which is everything the West Coast IPA isn't: soft on the palate, low in bitterness, murky in appearance, with a very discreet malt presence and a singular, almost overwhelming juiciness, guided by hop strains like Citra and Mosaic.

The East Coast IPA is still in its adolescence. The Alchemist's Heady Topper, brewed in Waterbury, Vermont, is often cited as one of the forefathers of the style, and was first released in its distinctive silver cans in 2011. Today, a coterie of East Coast breweries – including Tree House, Trillium, Bissell Brothers, Tired Hands, and many more – are turning out key exemplars of the style.

What's next for the IPA, then? The East Coast IPA is still ascending, and will likely be the subject of great excitement for years to come. But if there's any single takeaway, it's that the IPA remains one of the most dynamic, exciting and versatile styles in craft beer – and its ongoing evolution is all but guaranteed.

"THE IPA REMAINS ONE OF THE MOST DYNAMIC, EXCITING, AND VERSATILE STYLES IN CRAFT BEER"

TERROIR IN BEER

Terroir may be a concept that's borrowed from the wine world, but it's gaining new relevance for craft brewers and beer drinkers

Terroir is an idea that originates from the wine world. Its main premise: that the flavours, aromas, and other characteristics present in a wine are directly representative of where, and how, it was cultivated. From the nature of the soil to the regional climate and the amount of sun a given slope will receive, every viticultural element will have an impact on what ends up in the glass. Terroir is a wine's unique calling card.

But expressing terroir in beer is a far more complicated premise. Unlike wine, which is, for the most part, made exclusively with grapes and yeast, beer has many component parts. A single brew can feature malt produced in the UK alongside hops grown in New Zealand with fruit that hails from California, all fermented with a Belgian-born yeast strain. Given the carbon footprints implicit in using ingredients from across the globe, the idea that beer can express idiosyncratic locality may not be obvious.

And yet, there are ways that terroir is still relevant to the brewing process. Hops are one example. Just as Sauvignon Blanc grapes will taste profoundly different when planted in France than in South Africa, so individual hop varieties will differ in their aromatics depending on where in the world they're grown.

Cascade is an excellent case study. First bred in the US in 1956, the hop is famous for its role in helping to kick-start the American craft beer revolution. Drinkers know it for its distinctive grapefruit and citrus flavours, as well as its good bittering potential. But when Cascade hops were planted in New Zealand, they instead offered lime and tropical fruit aromatics – so much so that the New Zealand planting of the hop had to be renamed to Taiheke, because it didn't taste like classic Cascade.

Harvesting unique microflora for use in fermentation is another way that a brewery can express its local identity. Breweries like Cantillon in Brussels are famous for using coolships: large, open-top containers that hold freshly made wort, and which are designed to attract whatever wild yeast and bacteria are in the vicinity. Once inoculated and produced, the 'spontaneously fermented' beer is utterly unique; even a brewery ten miles away will have a different array of microflora. Previously a traditional brewing practice, the use of spontaneous fermentation is now being explored by a number of up-and-coming craft breweries, including De Garde in Tillamook, Oregon and Black Project in Denver, Colorado.

Then there are the breweries for which terroir is an abiding concept. Brouwerij Hof Ten Dormaal, a farmhouse brewery based in Tildonk, Belgium, offers an excellent example of terroir's role in beer. Not only do the brewers harvest wild yeast from Hof Ten Dormaal's immediate vicinity, they even grow their own grains, cultivate their own hops, and use their own well water. The result is a beer that is profoundly expressive of where it was produced; it also demonstrates how farmstead brewing can be a model of sustainability for the future.

That's just the start. From the rise of small, independent maltsters to the use of hand-foraged fruits, herbs, and other local ingredients in the brewing process, the idea of terroir in beer is only going to become more prominent, and more relevant, in the years to come.

WHY FRESH IS ALWAYS BEST... MOST OF THE TIME

Keep it cold, keep it dark and drink it fresh if you want to get the most out of your beer collection

Beer is a food product and as such should always be stored cold and consumed when it's as fresh as possible – well, most of the time anyway. Elsewhere in this book we'll explain why you might want to age some beers in your collection and the best way in which to do that but for now let's focus on why there's little point in hanging on to most of the beer you buy for too long.

Beer is made from fresh ingredients: fresh malt and grain, fresh water, fresh yeast and fresh hops. The longer elements such as heat, oxygen and time act on these ingredients the less enjoyment you'll be able to get out of them. Modern packaging technology has come a long way in defending beer from these elements and cans have become immensely popular in recent times as a result of brewers attempting to protect their creations. Cans are great because they protect beer from its external environment exceedingly well – don't discount the humble bottle though, as these are great too – with the exception being green and clear glass bottles that do not protect beer against UV light.

Craft beer has always prided itself on producing a product that is unfiltered and unpastuerised, as well as using ingredients, especially hops, in increasingly large amounts. The result of these processes in modern beer is a product that is far more volatile and as a result more susceptible to degradation over a shorter period of time. Storing your beer in a cool, dark place is always going to prolong its life, but never indefinitely.

Hops are a great starting point when looking at why freshness is important in beer. This is especially true with the prominence of aromatic pale ales and IPA that use 'dry hopping' as a technique to impart as much hop aroma and flavour into these beers as possible. Dry hopping involves adding hops either during or post-fermentation while the beer is cooled to a very low temperature in order to allow the yeast to drop out of the finished product naturally.

When hops are boiled, a component in the hops known as 'alpha acids' are broken down to create bitterness – but in dry hopping these long, yet fragile chains of molecules are left whole, adding aroma instead of bitterness. These volatile essential oils are easily broken down if the beer is not kept cold and over time the delightful citrus and tropical fruit aromas your beer once possessed will become tired and vegetal tasting. Oxygen, though, is perhaps a beer's worst enemy, quickly acting on the compounds within the beer to produce stale, musty, mouldy and even cardboardy flavours.

Breweries will do everything they can to avoid this happening to your beer, and that involves investing huge amounts of money in packaging technology and quality control – but one thing a brewery will never be in control of is time. Even the seals created by the best canning and bottling machines are not impervious and eventually, be it weeks, months or in some cases years, the beer you have spent your hard-earned money on will taste little like the brewer intended. So be good to your brewer and if they tell you to drink fresh, listen.

365 BEST BEERS IN THE WORLD

A YEAR OF GREAT BEER

Beer is the ultimate seasonal drink as anyone who's enjoyed a chilled pilsner in the height of summer or sipped a pint of stout by a warming fire in mid-winter will confirm. So we've selected the finest craft beers in the world and then organised them all seasonally to give you an idea of what to drink whether the autumn leaves are falling or it's the first flush of spring...

spring

It's time for ambitious plans, fresh ideas and enjoying winter's end. Pressing the restart button on your palate couldn't be easier. Cast off the heaviness of dark, wintery ales, and in their place grow the bright, citrus-strewn orchards of blonde beers, pale ales and IPAs. As the sun peeks through the clouds and things bloom out of winter's gloom, sip some fresh, invigorating, hoppy delights to accompany the first tempting thoughts of sunshine and warmth.

PALE ALE
SIERRA NEVADA PALE ALE
is a completely natural ale, brewed with the finest malted barley, whole-cone hops, brewer's yeast and pure water. Each bottle is conditioned naturally creating a more unique and flavorful ale.
Purest Ingredients
Finest Quality
SIERRA NEVADA
PALE ALE
ALC. 5.6% VOL.
350 mLe 35 cLe
BREWED & BOTTLED BY SIERRA NEVADA BREWING CO., CHICO, CA, U.S.A.
liny
Elder
RUSSIAN RIVER BREWING CO. SANTA ROSA
ALE 1 pint, 1.25 fl. oz. (510 ML)

CITRA

Sweetness and bitterness elegantly combined in a single bottle

Single-hopped beers are an increasingly common fixture in craft beer. They are particularly useful to people trying to learn more about flavours of specific hops, like a writer reading more books in a specific genre to understand it better. Every now and again, a brewer will use a hop that can do all the work on its own. Citra is such a hop, relatively high in the alpha acids that impart bitterness to beer, and full of citrusy aroma.

Oakham Ales claim to be the first British brewer to use the hop commercially, doing so back in 2009. Their Citra beer proved to be so popular it was brewed again, and again, before becoming a permanent fixture in 2011. A deep, shimmering gold, it pours with a tight and lively head that laces the glass nicely and smells absolutely divine. Its mouthwatering aroma offers grapefruit, lychee and lemons, with hardly any malt character detectable at all. This beer is a showcase for the hop, and what a hop it is.

The first sip is a mouth-puckering, palate-popping burst of soft, chewable fruit. A light malt base provides a simple biscuit base as the Citra hops march out all-singing, all-dancing. Rather than muddled bursts of different fruity, bitter flavours, Oakham Citra is a smooth, rolling wave of juicy grapefruit and lime that coats the tongue and leaves a sticky, resinous finish without becoming too cloying. The finish is quite sharp, quenching and dominated by grapefruit, but each sip offers a little more: peach, melon, papaya and juicy white grapes. There's no palate-stripping bitterness, but rather a lip-licking tartness that makes it enormously refreshing.

To see Oakham Citra really shine with food, try chicken breasts cooked in apricots and créme fraiche. The Citra gets in and under the creaminess and lifts up all the juicy fruit and savoury flavours. Citra is a stunning beer that never fails to astonish with its simple, subtle brilliance.

the facts

Brewer Oakham Ales
Origin Peterborough, UK
Strength 4.6%
Type Pale Ale
Web www.oakhamales.com
Temperature 8-12°C

REVIVAL

The moreish result of Somerset's refreshing magical alchemy

Moor Beer Company is based on an old dairy farm in Somerset, and has been steadily expanding and winning awards for their ales since 1996. They have seen a surge of popularity recently, and with fresh branding and awards under their belt, their beer is being enjoyed up and down the country. Revival was first brewed to celebrate the revival of the brewery, and it is one of the finest pale ales being made in the UK today.

Moor is also known for its 'unfined' beers, not using Isinglass finings to clear their beers, preferring a natural haze. As a result, Revival really shines, a beautiful, burnished gold with a slight, appetising cloudiness, sporting a thick, lasting head that laces the glass. This one's bottle-conditioned, so expect a lively pour from the hefty 660ml bottle.

Revival bursts with fresh, zesty, grapefruit and lime notes, and has a pleasing, spicy kick to your nostrils. All beers should be refreshing, but Revival really takes things to the next level. Its hop profile is a fizzing, citrus rocket that zooms around and around the palate. Fierce, bubbly grapefruit bursts in tandem with jabs of lemon, orange rind, a splash of pineapple. The finish is like lemon sherbet and key lime pie. Reviving is clearly its true purpose; in fact, its hop profile could probably wake the dead. It can't be stressed enough how sharp, juicy and smile-inducing this beer is.

Matching this beer to anything fruity would simply dilute the perfect citrus character. Instead, consider using it to cut through and enhance light, soft cheeses, while its carbonation and fresh zing is equally suited to the crunchy skin of moist, roast chicken.

Revival is simply invigorating. For a 4% beer, the flavours it boasts suggest some sort of magical alchemy is taking place down in Somerset, and Revival is utterly shaming to many ales of similar strength.

the facts

Brewer Moor Beer Company
Origin Somerset, UK
Strength 4%
Type Pale Ale
Web www.moorbeer.co.uk
Temperature 8-12°C

JARL

A modern, citrus twist on the traditional session ale

Fyne Ales in Argyll produce a core range of clean, balanced beers with real flavour and character. They also like to dabble in specialities and one-offs, but there are few brewers in the UK better than Fyne at making fantastic, flavourful, standard strength beers, especially on cask. Their bottled beers are just as good. Whilst the name of the brewery is apt, given their skill for clean, bright and delicious beers, it in fact refers to the location of the brewery near Loch Fyne in Argyll.

Another example of a single-hopped beer using Citra, Jarl is a golden ale, rather than a pale ale, and is named after the Jarls (Norse Earls) who raided and claimed much of that area of Scotland. Jarl's lighter malt body, close to a lager's, makes it an extremely easy-drinking session beer that still has the flavour muscles to satisfy in small quantities. So much so in fact, that Jarl won the Champion Beer of Scotland at the 2013 Scottish Real Ale Festival and was also crowned Champion Golden Ale at the 2013 Great British Beer Festival.

Jarl uses extra pale malt to achieve its straw-like pale gold colour, and its generous head is a fascinating bouquet of citrus and tropical fruit, particularly kiwi and grapefruit, and fresh biscuits. The relatively light body never seems thin, thanks to an even, mouth-filling fruitiness that is both soft and juicy. Rather than an assertive grapefruit character, Jarl displays a fruitness more like kiwi and white grapes, with a touch of grapefruit and lemon in the soft, long finish.

It's a remarkably balanced beer that is ideal for warm days in the garden and enjoying with light meals. Try a plate of mild cheddars, grapes and slices of pear on some warm white rolls, or a crispy-coated chicken burger with lime mayo to enjoy the unpretentious and deliciously simple hop character of this extremely modern session ale.

the facts

Brewer Fyne Ales
Origin Argyll, Scotland, UK
Strength 3.8%
Type Golden Ale
Web www.fyneales.com
Temperature 8-12°C

THE BEER TALKING

MALCOLM DOWNIE
BREWER AT FYNE ALES

What was the inspiration behind Jarl?
The beer initially came about as a summer special - our previous head brewer had sourced a small quantity of Citra from the first batch that came across from the US. Popular demand decided that when the next season's crop became available, we bought a lot more! The name is a wee nod to our previous summer special Somerled. He was the guy who drove the Vikings out of the West of Scotland. Our subsequent summer special, Rune, also takes a tilt at this line of thought.

Which beer best defines who Fyne Ales are as a brewery?
I'd say Jarl - golden, hoppy beers are a massive part of what we brew. It's got a lot of flavour, but it's well balanced and easy drinking, which is pretty much what we strive for in all our beers!

NW DIPA EKUANOT

A punchy, assertive, and deliciously potent double IPA

THE FACTS
Brewer Cloudwater Brew Co
Origin Manchester, UK
Strength 9%
Type Double IPA
Web www.cloudwaterbrew.co/
Temperature 6-8°C

In 2016, Cloudwater was named RateBeer's fifth-best brewery in the world. That achievement isn't a surprise. From the get-go, Cloudwater's IPAs – brewed largely following the East Coast model, hazy, almost absurdly aromatic, and flavourful – made palpable the brewery's talent and ambitions.

One of several leading British breweries that have made the call to eschew a core range in favour of developing a steady stream of new recipes, Cloudwater was also aware, early, of the role that optics had to play in selling beer. Every new release came plastered with a colourful, one-off label illustrated by a local artist, first in bottles and then in silver tallboy cans.

Consequently, every time a new double IPA was released as part of Cloudwater's 'v' series, the crowds seeking cans grew in proportion. When the brewery announced that the series would conclude with v13 in early 2017, there was initial dismay followed by eagerness at what was to follow. Now, Cloudwater is moving forward with three variations on the stronger IPA style: the NW DIPA, the IIPA, and the NE DIPA.

The hallmark of the NW DIPA experimental strand is the use of a local JW Lees yeast strain, either alone or in tandem with one of Cloudwater's house yeasts. As with the prior 'v' series, each iteration of NW DIPA will be slightly different; this version centres on Ekuanot – formerly known as Equinox – a hop that derives from the Warrior hop. Rich in bitter alpha acids, it's also highly aromatic, and offers a gorgeous array of melon, papaya, pine, and bell pepper flavours. As a showcase for this exciting new hop, this DIPA excels. And as an indication of what's next for Cloudwater, it bodes very well indeed.

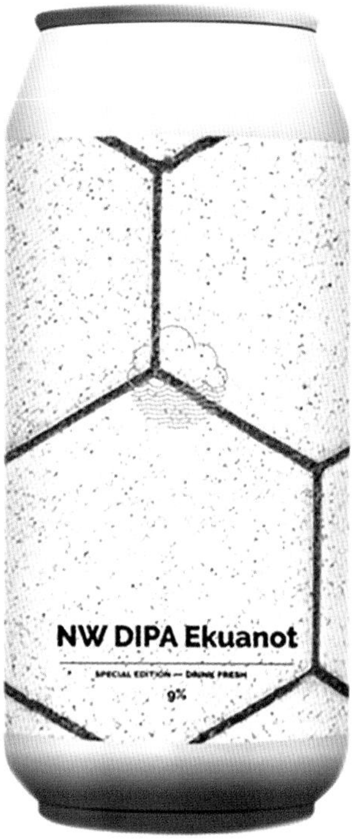

MARBLE BITTER

The freshest cask beer to come out of a bottle

THE FACTS
Brewer Marble Brewery
Origin Manchester, UK
Strength 4.2%
Type Bitter
Web www.marblebeers.com
Temperature 8-12°C

The Marble Brewery was established in Manchester in 1997 as a means of saving The Marble Arch Inn from closing down. Fortunately, they made the right choice, and after more than a decade of brewing, Marble were noticed on the wider craft beer scene. The 12-barrel brewery now struggles to meet popular demand for their beers, which range from the no-nonsense-named Pint to the groundbreaking Earl Grey IPA.

Manchester Bitter is Marble's best-selling beer and is sold in cask and bottle across the UK. However, the popularity began when it was being sold from The Marble Arch Inn. It captured the interest of Mancunians because it was a beer that perfectly portrayed the Manchester preference for bitter, golden ales with mountains of creamy head.

Manchester Bitter has a golden hued brilliance and enough foamy white head to ski on. It almost gives cask beer a run for its money when it comes to being fresh and lively. The aroma is understated but full of charm, with lemon meringue, sharp lime zest and gentle lavender coming through.

The body is as energetic and lively as they come; it genuinely swells and fizzes in the mouth. If you take long enough to let the head fade down all it takes is a quick swirl in the glass to rouse up a fresh avalanche of foam. The taste is refreshingly bitter, with clean citrus rind, pineapple and dry grain flavours and a bittersweet, floral hop finish.

This is the exact beer needed to blow off the corporate cobwebs after a long day at work and to revitalise body and soul for the evening ahead.

LITTLE CREATURES PALE ALE

A laid-back pale ale full of creamy tropical fruit flavours

The hop vine is a cousin of the cannabis plant, and the cones used for brewing are made up of oily, pungent green leaves. Sometimes, all it takes is a drink as innocent-looking as Little Creatures Pale Ale to make you sit back and marvel at what the humble hop leaf can achieve. This Australian pale ale pours light amber with a modest white head and as soon as you move in to take that first sip, a fresh burst of green mango greets you, with lychee and dragon fruit joining in to form an exotic fruit salad aroma.

The brewers don't chuck whole mangoes into the fermenting vat or top up the bottles with fruit juice – all of these bright, tropical aromas come from the hops. Those wonderful little leaves, you just want to eat them right up. Don't. They taste awful, unlike Little Creatures, which has a mango and passion fruit ice cream taste up front, seasoned with a touch of vanilla. A crunchy, luscious malt base lifts it up, lending additional brown sugar and caramel sweetness. The crisp, bitter finish reassures drinkers that this is a beer and not a glass of fruit cocktail syrup.

It sounds intense but, compared with many pale ales and IPAs from the United States, there's a relaxed, Pacific island feel to Little Creatures. It's gentle, refreshing, uplifting, and gone all too quickly. The hallmark of a good beer is its adaptability, and Little Creatures ticks a lot boxes – it wouldn't be out of place at a barbecue, a party, as the post-work drink or simply a quiet evening in.

If you think Australian beer is just Foster's and Castlemaine, Little Creatures Pale Ale will readjust your world view in the best possible way. It was the beer they launched with in 2001 and its success has enabled them to open up another brewery, a bar and a 'dining hall'.

the facts

Brewer Little Creatures Brewing Party
Origin Fremantle, Australia
Strength 5.2%
Flavour Mango, passion fruit and caramel
Web https://littlecreatures.com.au
Temperature 4-8°C

MARY JANE

A supremely versatile Yorkshire pale ale, suited to any occasion

The English county of Yorkshire already punches well above its weight in beer terms, with more breweries than either London or Wales, and a worldwide reputation thanks to names such as Samuel Smith. Nevertheless, the fine folk of Yorkshire aren't content to rest on their past glories, and young blood breweries have come out with their fists swinging to ensure Yorkshire remains at the forefront of the British brewing scene.

Amongst these is the modern Ilkley Brewery, which opened in 2009. It continues the legacy of the Ilkley Brewery and Aerated Water Company which shut down in the 1920s. Since 2009, Ilkley has brewed more than 25 beers, some of them weirdly exotic brews, such as Siberia, a rhubarb saison, and the Mayan, a chilli chocolate beer. With such curious relatives, a pale ale could be easily overlooked, but fortunately that's not the case and Mary Jane is still its best-selling flagship beer.

It has a bright, clear gold appearance and a tight, white head. Cascade and Amarillo hops from the United States impart a floral blossom and pithy orange rind aroma respectively. The Maris Otter and Crystal malts lend the faintest hint of malty Ovaltine in the background.

The orange bite of the Amarillo hop, backed up by Cascade's grapefruit zest, forms the main thrust of Mary Jane's flavour. An off-handed right hook of malty Ovaltine comes through towards the end, before a quick upper-cut of sweet, Scottish shortbread biscuit lands the finishing blow. It's all delivered quickly, with a dancer's art and precision, leaving you quietly impressed.

Mary Jane is delicious without being hop intense, making for a very versatile beer. It's one to enjoy on its own, with fish and chips, with friends or with a newspaper, to savour or sink quickly.

the facts

Brewer Ilkley Brewery
Origin North Yorkshire, UK
Strength 3.5%
Type Pale Ale
Web www.ilkleybrewery.co.uk
Temperature 10-12°C

YANKEE

A modern classic of the Pale Ale style and one of the most well-balanced beers on the market

Rooster's is another of the great, modern Yorkshire breweries to rise up in recent years. They've been brewing for over 20 years now, which can seem surprising as their approach is still as fresh and modern as any new micro-brewery.

When they first started, the British ale market was dominated by bitter and brown beers, so they set out to do something different – create a pale ale. It's almost impossible to imagine a brewery regarding pale ale as 'something different' today, and Rooster's claim it was Yankee that helped kick off the modern trend in the UK. Rooster's imported US hops for their beers and the American influence seeped through into their all-American beer names: as well as Yankee there's the likes of Fort Smith, True Grit and Wild Mule.

Yankee is genuinely magnificent on cask and worth seeking out especially if you're in Yorkshire; nevertheless, it's still a cracking beer from the bottle. It pours with the colour of freshly polished brass, a bright, shining beer with just a touch of haze and capped by a tight, white head.

The aroma is floral, with fresh cut grass and a boisterous depth of malt. Rooster's pride themselves on delivering hop-forward ales. In today's hop-obsessed craft beer market that's what catches attention but they really should shout louder about their malt and water combination.

The clean, soft water profile enhances the malt, creating a subtle depth of cereal, sugary biscotti, and a touch of smoke. By today's face-peeling, hop-bomb standards, there's a risk of viewing something like Yankee as tame, but that would be foolish. It's brilliantly well-balanced, with every component playing a key part, the water boosting the hops and malt, the malt giving depth and body, and the hops providing a floral aroma and citrus bite.

the facts

Brewer Rooster's
Origin Yorkshire, UK
Strength 4.3%
Type Pale Ale
Web www.roosters.co.uk
Temperature 12°C

ZOMBIE DUST

Boldly tropical, pleasingly dank, and ultimately, beautifully balanced

Say the name '3 Floyds' to most beer geeks, and the first thing they'll think of is Dark Lord Day. One of the most anticipated events in the US beer calendar, Dark Lord Day celebrates the annual release of the brewery's heavily hyped Russian imperial stout, which is brewed with coffee, Mexican vanilla, and Indian sugar. Detractors scoff at the frenzy; devotees would make Faustian pacts to get their hands on the $180 tickets (and the four bottles of Dark Lord, plus one bottle of a Dark Lord variant, that each guarantees).

Sturm und drang aside, Dark Lord isn't the only 3 Floyds beer that's worth getting excited about. In fact, it's the more widely available Zombie Dust that, one could argue, best represents the brewery's chops, ambitions, and place in the zeitgeist.

Formerly known as Cenotaph, the beer was reborn as Zombie Dust after a partnership with, as the brewery says, "our marvellous friends in the comic industry." It's a brew that is apparently best consumed during the zombie apocalypse; its name also doubles as the term for the narcotic cocktail of cocaine and triazolam.

Where potency is concerned, it's true that Zombie Dust falls outside the typical alcohol content range specified for an American pale ale; at 6.2%, it could fairly be classed as an IPA (that tendency towards the softening of a relatively potent brew is perhaps evidence of 3 Floyds' propensity for sign-of-the-horns-style bigness and boldness in all things).

But it's also a phenomenally balanced beer, with a sweet, bready, caramel base offset by pineapple, lashings of mango, and, most crucially, a beguiling savoury note, a funk of onion and garlic. That can be chalked up to Zombie Dust's reliance on one single hop: Citra. Though a Citra-only beer may not stir drinkers in a post-Mosaic world the way it once would have, the exceptional Zombie Dust still serves as a delicious showcase for all that this versatile hop can accomplish.

Facts

Brewer 3 Floyds Brewing Co.
Origin Munster, Indiana, USA
Strength 6.2%
Type American Pale Ale
Web www.3floyds.com/
Temperature 6-8°C

GAMMA RAY

Rich with bold, juicy flavours and a quenching bitterness

Would it be an exaggeration to say that Gamma Ray – in its resplendent, spaceman-bedecked, blue-and-orange cans – single-handedly transformed London's craft beer scene when it made its debut in 2013? Perhaps, but only slightly. Against the backdrop of what had come before, the beer was juicy in all the right places, buoyant with tropical hops, boasted a moreish, lingering bitterness, and had the good looks to match. That it became a hit seems, in retrospect, hardly surprising.

Beavertown has the kind of romantic backstory that other breweries might long for. Picture a small barbecue restaurant in an unlikely corner of Hackney and a tiny 4BBL brew kit. (Picture, too, founder Logan Plant, son of *that* Robert Plant – rock and roll royalty is never a bad thing to add to one's origin story.) Still, Beavertown's beginnings were humble, and Gamma Ray wasn't one of the first on its roster. Earlier brews instead included the likes of Smog Rocket (a richly smoked porter) and Neck Oil (which began life as a bitter before recipe tweaks transformed it into the crisp and refreshing session IPA it is today).

When Gamma Ray landed, it was at exactly the right time to stir up a minor frenzy among London's beer drinkers, who were cultivating a taste for juicy, hop-driven styles. It was an instant smash, with a hop bill (Citra, Amarillo, Calypso, Columbus, and Bravo) that leaned towards the tropical but supplied a decent slug of bitterness, too.

Today, Gamma Ray is Beavertown's flagship, a star of its core range, and certainly part of the reason the brewery has since expanded to its sizeable headquarters in Tottenham Hale. It may no longer be the new kid on the block, but Gamma's status as a trailblazer means that London beer drinkers will likely never lose affection for their hometown hero.

the facts

Brewer Beavertown Brewery
Origin London, UK
Strength 5.4%
Type American Pale Ale
Web www.beavertownbrewery.co.uk/
Temperature 6-8°C

GHOST SHIP

There's nothing ghoulish about this gorgeously juicy ale

Adnams, a brewer of traditional ales on England's east coast, has become increasingly interesting in the last few years, coinciding with the appointment of Master Brewer Fergus Fitzgerald as Head Brewer. Fitzgerald loves to explore the extremes of what beer can be, as well as excelling in brewing well-balanced, delicious 'everyday' beers. Ghost Ship is Adnams' highly-acclaimed pale ale, brewed using Chinook, Columbus and Citra hops, and is just as delicious in a can as it is in the bottle.

A gorgeous amber colour, brassy at the edges, it displays tell-tale signs of the quality malts used, in particular the coppery whirlpool that forms in the glass as you pour it. Pale malt, spicy-sweet rye crystal malt and toffee-tasting cara malts have been used, all of which contribute to a warming, slightly spicy, toasty, honey aroma, enhanced by the orange, grapefruit and floral notes added by the hops.

Ghost Ship has a juicy, citric sweetness that tingles the tongue like freshly squeezed fruit juice. It's never that tart though, instead starting out syrupy and honey-like, before the toasty body gives way to the apricot, peach and pink grapefruit. It ends with a firm but not aggressively bitter finish, pithy like orange peel. There are several beers that can boast the quenching range of flavours of Ghost Ship, but not nearly as many that stay fresh all the way through.

Whilst it's perfectly capable of satisfying the palate on its own, Ghost Ship is great with certain foods as well. Lightly spiced jerked meats, cheesy quesadillas and Chinese lemon-and-honey chicken are the order of the day for this zingy, citrusy and super-fresh beer. It enhances sweetness and spice, cutting through fat like a pirate's cutlass and adding a syrupy, fruity glaze to everything it touches. It's a superb, juicy and pithy pale ale, worthy of all the praise it gets.

the facts

Brewer Adnams
Origin Southwold, UK
Strength 4.5%
Type Pale Ale
Web www.adnams.co.uk
Temperature 8-12°C

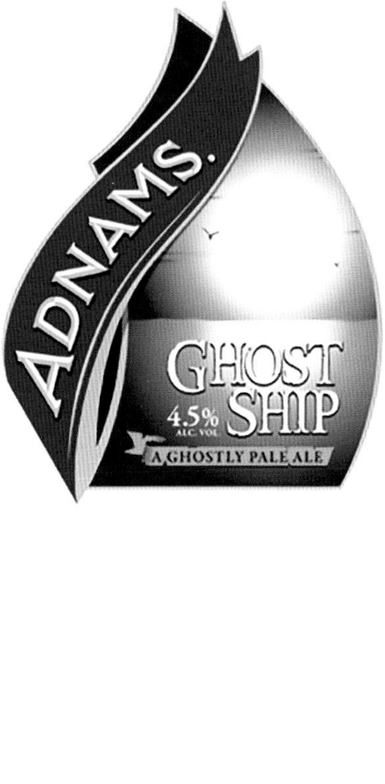

NELSON

Alpine Beer Company,San Diego, California, USA
Type American IPA Strength 7%

It's not just the Kiwis that produce stunning beers with the magical Nelson Sauvin hop – as you might imagine the Americans are pretty handy with it themselves. Alpine Nelson is one of those 'must seek out' beers if you're ever in California. It reeks of the tropical fruit and vinous quality that makes Nelson Sauvin so sought after by brewers before twisting around your throat with a resinous finish.

PALE RIDER

Kelham Island, UK
Type Pale Ale Strength 5.2%

If you're thinking about moving from lager into ale then this Champion Beer of Britain is a good reason to make the switch and probably the best place to start. Dave Wickett initially brewed Pale Rider with the aim of encouraging female drinkers to switch from lager to ale, but it soon found success with everyone and it now stands as their best-selling beer. It is made with plenty of aromatic hops and fewer bittering hops, which serves to give it a pleasant, floral aroma and a taste with minimal bitterness in the finish.

RACER 5

Bear Republic Brewing Company, Cloverdale, California, USA
Type American IPA Strength 7.5%

It's uncertain as to whether or not this beer is so named because of how fast it disappears from your glass when it's put in front of you. What is certain is that the fusion of American Columbus and Cascade hops along with delicately sweet, biscuit malts combine to make one of the finest IPAs in the US. Expect notes of grapefruit with a hint of caramel up front, followed by a resinous and slightly grassy finish.

LUPULOID

Beavertown Brewery, London, UK
Type American IPA Strength 6.7%

It took Beavertown four years to make a traditional IPA. The North London brewery first made its name with brews like Gamma Ray, a much-celebrated American Pale Ale, and Neck Oil Session IPA – but Lupuloid was well worth the wait. Cloudy and redolent of tropical fruits but tempered with a moderate bitterness, the beer is lent a touch of earthy pungency courtesy of Mosaic and Citra hops.

HOPHEAD

Dark Star, West Sussex, UK
Type Pale Ale Strength 3.8%

Hophead is never as hoppy as you might hope from the name. Instead it's a light to medium-bodied, floral golden ale with delicately blended flavours of grapefruit, lemon, fresh cut grass and malt. The finish is well balanced and bittersweet. Forget the name though, it's a thirst-quenching session ale designed for pub beer gardens.

THE CREAM ALE

Anspach & Hobday, London, UK
Type Cream Ale Strength 5.2%

Traditionally, a Cream Ale utilises maize (or corn for our American friends) in addition to malted barley, adding a lighter body, not unlike a lager, to this beer style. Anspach & Hobday fuse the drinkability of its Cream Ale with Sorachi Ace hops, adding notes of mango and lemongrass to this incredibly quaffable beer.

TWO HEARTED ALE

Bell's Brewing, Kalamazoo, Michigan, USA
Type American IPA Strength 7%

It only takes a single sip to realise why Bell's Two Hearted Ale is revered amongst beer lovers. Two Hearted is just about the perfect example of an American IPA, fusing together familiar notes of grapefruit and pine that are balanced by a touch of sweetness from the malt and a satisfyingly bitter finish. It's a beer that's often imitated and seldom matched.

WITCHSHARK

Bellwood's Brewery, Toronto, Canada
Type Double IPA Strength 9%

Is it a witch or is it a shark? That's really of no consequence – this beer from Canada's Bellwood's Brewery is a superb example of a modern double IPA. Witchshark stacks wave after wave of North American hop flavours on top of each other, producing mango, lychee and pine in spades before leading to an intense yet satisfying bitter finish.

LANDLORD

Timothy Taylor, Yorkshire, UK
Type Pale Ale Strength 4.3%

Timothy Taylor has been brewing since 1858, drawing on soft water Pennine spring water for its traditional beers. Landlord is their flagship ale, having won CAMRA's Champion Beer of Britain award four times, and Madonna claimed it was her favourite ale. It's marmalade hued, presenting a delicate citrus and floral aroma. The taste is balanced between citrusy hops and biscuit malt that leads to a bitter, lemony finish.

RE ALE

Birra del Borgo, Italy
Type Pale Ale Strength 6.4%

Italy is experiencing its own craft beer Renaissance, and Leonardo Di Vincenzo of Birra del Borgo is one of the nation's new brewing artists. With more of a grape than a grain culture in Italy, Di Vincenzo draws his inspiration from British beer, and Re Ale is an Italian take on the classic British bitter. It has a grapefruit aroma, spicy orange marmalade taste and crisp bitter finish.

LUX

Bissell Brothers Brewing Company, Portland, Maine, USA
Type Rye Ale Strength 5.1%

Lux's 1980's pink-and-blue can jars somewhat with the idea of a sweet, spicy rye ale, but it's all about texture. Rye helps provide the chewy backbone to a palate-soaking combination of guava, lychee and passion fruit, stopping the hops from wearing out your palate and making each mouthful as smooth as yacht-rock.

SWISH

Bissell Brothers Brewing Company, Portland, Maine, USA
Type Double IPA Strength 8%

A fast-rising star in the New England brewing scene, Bissell Brothers turns out the kind of hazy, unctuous IPAs for which the region is famous. And Swish is one of the brewery's most coveted cans. A zeitgeisty hop bill (Mosaic, Citra, Simcoe, and Apollo) makes this a distinctly savoury beer, with allium notes at the fore; ample tropical fruit flavours add to this powerful punch of a DIPA.

NOTORIOUS

Boneyard Beer, Bend, Oregon, USA
Type Triple IPA Strength 11.5%

Bombastic, bodacious, but artfully balanced, Boneyard's Notorious is a world-class example of a triple IPA. Though it measures in at a hefty 11.5% ABV, the beer integrates its alcohol beautifully – no lingering heat impinges on its surprising drinkability. Jammy without being cloying, malt-driven without being overly sweet, its bouquet of irresistible tropical fruit, citrus, and pine notes, inspires flights of rapture.

INSANE RUSH IPA

Bootstrap Brewing, Niwot, Colorado, USA
Type American IPA Strength 7.6%

Niwot is a small town just outside of Boulder, Colorado and it's home to a brewery that might just be one of the state's best-kept secrets. Bootstrap Brewing produces a range of incredibly stylish and accomplished beers for such a small operation and the highlight is surely Insane Rush. This modern, yet bitter IPA melds juicy notes of mango with bitter lemon peel, leaving a lingering bitterness on the palate.

05|11 IPA CITRA & MOSAIC

Brew By Numbers, London, UK
Type American IPA Strength 6.9%

At first glance Brew By Numbers' beer labelling system might seem a little confusing but it's simple enough to work out. When you do have it figured out you'll know that the numbers 05|11 mean that one of the best IPAs in its range is back. Huge amounts of Citra and Mosaic hops deliver pithy citrus, tropical and dank, savoury aromas, with a delicate pale malt backdrop keeping things in check while the hops shine.

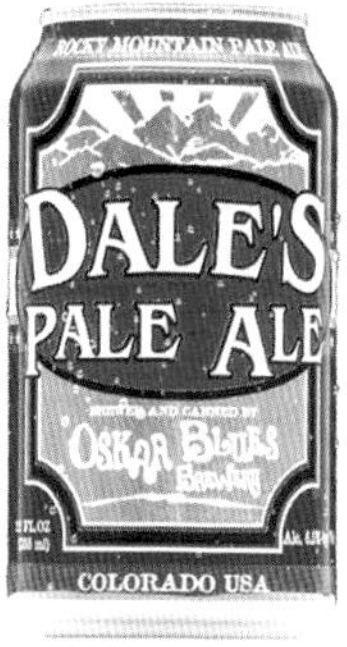

DALE'S PALE ALE

Oskar Blues, Colorado, USA
Type Pale Ale Strength 6.5%

Canned craft beer is already a big deal in the United States and it's starting to catch on in the UK, mainly through US imports but also with the efforts of breweries like BrewDog. Packed full of hops, Dale's Pale Ale is an amber colour beer with tons of resiny pine and citrus aromas, and a sweet caramel taste balanced by grapefruit, lemon and pine.

MANGOFEBER DIPA (1)

Brewski, Helsingborg, Sweden
Type Fruit Double IPA Strength 8%

• The prototypical Double IPA in 2017 is marked by its juiciness, by its aromatics, and by its preponderance of exotic fruit flavours. That Sweden's Brewski has opted to dose its DIPA with actual chunks of mango, then, is hardly a stretch. Accompanied by Amarillo and Mosaic hops, and tempered by a good amount of bitterness, it's a love letter to the tropics.

FAT & FRUITY (2)

Dry & Bitter Brewing Company, Gørløse, Denmark
Type American IPA Strength 6.5%

• Seen by the Danish brewery as a sister beer to its Dank & Juicy IPA, Fat & Fruity has clear New England IPA influences, with oats and wheat contributing to its hazy appearance and smooth mouthfeel. A heavy dry hopping of Citra, Ekuanot, Mosaic and Simcoe make for a mouth-watering tropical aroma, and a palate soaked with peach, mandarin and mango.

SURF WAX IPA

Burial Beer Co, Asheville, North Carolina, USA
Type American IPA Strength 6.8%

• From its one-barrel beginnings in 2013 to its status today as one of Asheville's highlight breweries, Burial Beer Co. has blossomed into a true cult favourite. The brew to begin with is its flagship Surf Wax IPA. Hazy orange in the glass, this delightfully dank IPA is also heavy on the bold fruit flavours, making for a moreish balance of sweet and savoury.

PERMANENT DAYLIGHT

Cellarmaker Brewing Co, San Francisco, California, USA
Type American IPA Strength 6.4%

• Cellarmaker burst onto the Northern California brewing scene in 2013, quickly building a reputation for itself on the back of accomplished pale and hop forward beers. Its flagship IPA, Permanent Daylight, packs in flavours of passion fruit, gooseberry and grapefruit pith. It's so tasty that it often tends to sell out on the day of its release.

PALE FIRE

Pressure Drop, London UK
Type Pale Ale Strength 5.1%

• Pressure Drop are trying different hop combinations with each bottling of this beer. The latest version of this gloriously sharp and citric pale ale uses the sinister sounding British hop prototype, Hop X. There's nothing dark about the beer though – it's a shining, hazy gold, oozing with the scent of pulpy tropical fruits and honeyed lemon. Each taste is just as sharp, orangey and lemony as the one before it.

LAGUNITAS (3)

Lagunitas Brewing Co., California USA
Type Pale Ale Strength 6.2%

• Lagunitas' Pale Ale is subtitled New Dogtown as it was concocted after the move to their larger premises. A very pale amber, closer to burnished gold, with a rich, apricot aroma accented with lychee and golden-syrup-cookies. It's a fierce, angry beast, and comes racing into your face with a pawful of apricot hand grenades. It dries out in the finish, the grenades exploding harmlessly and deliciously into shrapnel of lemons and lychee.

JAI ALAI

Cigar City Brewing, Tampa, Florida, USA
Type American IPA Strength 7.5%

• Jai Alai is an American IPA that takes its name from a ball game played in the Basque region of Spain – it was also once played in Tampa, Florida where this accomplished IPA hails from, hence why it earned this name. Jai Alai is no longer played in Tampa, but this beer remains in its stead, packed with notes of caramel, grapefruit flesh with a pine sap bitterness in the finish. A true classic.

TROPICALIA (4)

Creature Comforts Brewing Co, Athens, Georgia, USA
Type American IPA Strength 6.6%

• If you ever get the chance to visit the United States, do yourself a favour and visit the Peach State. Georgia is home to some of the country's best up-and-coming breweries, including Athens' Creature Comforts. Among its accomplished core range is Tropicalia, an IPA in the modern style which lets juicy, tropical fruit flavours shine before slowing, panning out with a soft, balanced finish.

STEADY ROLLING MAN (5)

DEYA Brewing Company, Cheltenham, UK
Type Pale Ale Strength 5.2%

• New kids on the block, DEYA Brewing Company specialise in hoppy, hazy, modern beer styles. Its flagship pale ale Steady Rolling Man epitomises the Cheltenham-based brewery's irreverent attitude. Steady Rolling Man fuses North American hops to form a heady, hazy cocktail that's bursting with ripe flavours of citrus and tropical fruit. It's very difficult to only have one.

MORALITE (6)

Brasserie Dieu du Ciel!, Montreal, Canada
Type American IPA Strength 6.9%

• Beginning life as a Montreal brewpub in 1998, Dieu du Ciel! quickly developed a reputation for experimental, uncompromising beers. Moralité, an IPA first brewed in collaboration with Vermont's The Alchemist, is a gutsy, energetic IPA, its aroma packed with pineapple, mango and citrus. The fruit-forward palate hides its strength, while its resinous, bitter finish leaves the drinker thirsty for more.

TATERS

Other Half Brewing Co, New York, USA
Type Pale Ale Strength 5.5%

• One of a series of collaborations between Other Half and Monkish (including Twice Baked Potato, and Fully Loaded Baked Potato, which also involved Trillium), Taters' grainbill is heavily loaded with oats, for a mouthfeel that's thick and silky. A double dry-hopping of Australian Enigma and New Zealand Riwaka hops makes for a tropical smoothie of passion fruit, pineapple and grapefruit.

NEW ZEALAND PALE ALE

Hawkshead Brewery, Cumbria, UK
Type Pale Ale Strength 6%

• A shimmering, burnished gold beer, bright and appetising with a well-built head. The aroma has a rugged, spicy intensity. The flavours are really fresh kiwi, grapes, bitter orange pith, overlaying a thick, syrupy body that stays quaffable somehow, with the judicious application of fast, sharp citric jabs to lift it just above the palate. Further on, things get sticky and resinous with bitterness, but only in a way that makes you even thirstier.

SUMMER LIGHTNING

Hop Back Brewery, Salisbury, Wiltshire UK
Type Pale Ale Strength 5%

• In 1986, Exmoor Gold put the cat among the pigeons with their revolutionary pale ale, unseen in British pubs since the days of India Pale Ales. But in 1988 it was Hop Back's Summer Lightning that ensured pale ale wasn't a passing fad. Single hopped with East Kent Goldings, it is full of summery floral, fresh cut grass and citrus aromas, with bittersweet lemon and lime flavours that linger on a long, drying finish.

HOP ZOMBIE (7)

Epic, Auckland, New Zealand
Type Double IPA Strength 8%

• New Zealand is home to one of the most mature modern beer cultures in the world. However, this beer from Auckland's Epic is anything but – instead it could be described as brash, arrogant and in your face. Hop Zombie uses heaps upon heaps of aromatic US hops to produce a heady, bitter beer chock full of grapefruit, lemon pith and pine notes with an ABV of 8% that is barely detectable.

MANGO MANGO MANGO (8)

Dugges Bryggeri & Stillwater Artisanal Ales, Landvetter, Sweden & Baltimore, USA
Type Fruit Sour Ale Strength 4.5%

• One of several collaboration brews that Dugges Bryggeri has made with Stillwater Artisanal Beer, Mango Mango Mango is a sour beer with an unabashed affinity for the fruit. Two different varieties of mangoes are used to impart that touch of tropicalia, while Mosaic hops, which are well known for their own exotic fruit profile, serve as the third addition.

EPIPHANY (9)

Foundation Brewing Company, Portland, Maine, USA
Type Double IPA Strength 8%

• Portland, Oregon may be famous as a beer lover's capital, but Portland, Maine is also earning acclaim for its lively brewing scene. One of the must-try breweries is Foundation. Begin with the Epiphany, a Double IPA that's brewed with Foundation's house strain of British ale yeast. Bright with grapefruit and guava flavours, it's also tempered with some resinous dankness.

IIPA

Pirate Life Brewing, Adelaide, Australia
Type Double IPA Strength 8.8%

• Instantly proving that whatever the Americans can do the Aussies can match, Pirate Life's IIPA provides an explosion of West Coast IPA flavour. A hefty hop bill featuring Centennial, Columbus, Simcoe and Mosaic ushers in potent aromas of pine, candied orange, melon and grapefruit zest. You'll find plenty of orange meets lemon fruit character on the palate, leading to a savoury finish of onions and chives.

GODZONE BEAT (10)

Fork Brewing, Wellington, New Zealand
Type New Zealand IPA Strength 5.9%

• Wellington is the beating heart at the centre of New Zealand's modern craft beer movement. Fork Brewing, and its home at the Fork & Brewer brewpub, is a shining example within this movement and its flagship IPA, Godzone Beat, pays homage to New Zealand hops. Nelson Sauvin, NZ Cascade and Pacific Jade imbue this beer with notes of orange peel, lychee and lime zest, ending with a fresh, grassy finish.

OF FOAM AND FURY

World-class West Coast DIPA from the west coast of Ireland

the facts

Brewer Galway Bay Brewery
Origin Galway, Ireland
Strength 8.5%
Type Double IPA
Web www.galwaybaybrewery.com
Temperature 6-8°C

Ireland's beer culture has been dominated by a single massive company and its dry stout for a very long time, but its craft beer scene, through years of hard work and occasionally a little subversive behaviour, has truly bloomed in the past few years. However, years before, breweries like Galway Bay were laying the groundwork for that scene, though not entirely intentionally.

Galway Bay Brewery began in 2009, started by Jason O'Connell and Niall Walsh as a way of suppling beer cheaply to their pub The Oslo in Galway. It was never intended to become a business spanning the country, but change was in the air and Galway Bay seemed perfectly placed to thrive. Crucially, the independence of Galway Bay's bars meant they had a showcase for their beers, without mainstream competitors on the bar beside them. The brewery now owns 11 different bars and produces some of Ireland's highest-rated beers. One of these is its Of Foam and Fury, a barnstorming, explosively fruity Double IPA.

It's a deep, orangey amber that suggests a potent malt backbone to bear the weight of its hop character, and its pungent aroma of passion fruit, pine and citrus really shows its dry hopping of Simcoe, Mosaic and Chinook. There's also a warming, marmalade-on-toast note in there which again suggests some sweetness.

Whilst it takes its inspiration from piney, dry American West Coast Double IPAs, there's a touch of red ale to this DIPA from the Irish west coast. Sticky with orange and caramel, boosted by a muscular, oily bitterness, its ripe fruitiness edged in sharp lime pith. It's a boisterous beer which isn't particularly interested in being subtle or understated: it's more of a shouted proclamation that Irish beer is changing, and you had better listen. Of course, this beer has your full attention from the very first sip.

PERNICIOUS WEED

An assault on the senses from bitter and aromatic New Zealand hops

Wellington, New Zealand has in recent years cemented itself as one of the greatest beer cities in the world. It's home to some of the best bars and brewpubs you can find not just in NZ, but the whole world. These include Hashigo Zake, Golding's Free Dive, Husk and Fork & Brewer among many others. Unsurprisingly it's also home to some ground-breaking, innovative breweries and perhaps the most prominent of these on the global stage is Garage Project.

You can find Garage Project's brewery on Aro Street, just outside of the city centre. There's a growler station for purchasing beer to go right by the brewery itself and just over the road is its taproom, with a comprehensive list of the brewery's beers on tap and a buzzing atmosphere to match. It's a shining example of just how mature the beer culture in Wellington has become.

Garage Project has worked closely with New Zealand hop growers since its inception in 2011. Its flagship double IPA, Pernicious Weed, is a homage to the pungent and flavoursome Rakau and Nelson Sauvin hop varieties grown on the country's South Island. Pernicious Weed is a riotously bitter beer but builds wave upon wave of New Zealand hop flavour before the wave breaks to unleash that bitterness. Expect huge aromas of gooseberry, passionfruit and freshly cut grass – not unlike a NZ Sauvignon Blanc – before flavours of grapefruit and lychee ride that wave all the way to this beer's finish. Despite its 8% ABV, it's also moreishly drinkable, which cements its status as one of the best beers being produced in the world at this moment.

the facts

Brewer Garage Project
Origin Wellington, New Zealand
Strength 8%
Type Double IPA
Web www.garageproject.co.nz
Temperature 6-8°C

JAIPUR

This refreshing bottle is Britain's most highly awarded beer and it's not hard to see why

The Thornbridge Brewery is one of the most acclaimed and respected breweries in Britain. They started in the outbuildings of Thornbridge Hall, a stately home in the Peak District, and given the natural elegance of their beers and styling, you can imagine them having been there for centuries. Impressively, they've only been around since 2005, and opened a new site in the nearby town of Bakewell in 2009 to meet demand.

A very crucial part of this success is Jaipur, which is now being brewed in excess of two million pints per year. It was first made in 2005 back when BrewDog boss Martin Dickie worked for Thornbridge, and you can see his hand at work. Jaipur looks to the States for its influence, containing Ahtanum, Centennial and Chinook hops. This is no US clone, though; the Maris Otter malt profile guarantees a sharp bitterness that's entirely British. The British have taken to this fusion of American hops and local outlook, with Jaipur having won over 100 worldwide awards to date.

It pours a very pale gold and clear colour with a generous, bright white head. The aroma is delightfully crisp, clean and energising, a wake-up call of lemon and grapefruit paired with subtle woody, pine notes. These refreshing citrus flavours are sharp and outspoken from the first sip. The attentive listener might hear the distant cry of a sweet honey note; otherwise the citrus taste ramps up the bitterness towards a lingering lime finish.

Jaipur has been named in the Guild of Fine Foods top 50 food and drink products. On its own it's a fantastic summer refresher, but paired with food it suddenly opens up. Thornbridge have released a book titled *Craft Union* which explores the potential of their beers alongside food in depth. It's worth hunting down a copy and spending Sunday in the kitchen with a half case of Jaipur.

the facts

Brewer Thornbridge
Origin Bakewell, UK
Strength 5.9%
Type IPA
Web www.thornbridgebrewery.co.uk
Temperature 10-12°C

THE BEER TALKING

ROB LOVATT THORNBRIDGE BREWERY

What made you want to become a brewer?
Brewing was just something I had a natural affinity for. I loved the creative aspects of brewing, making something by hand from scratch and then enjoying the results.

What do you most enjoy about brewing?
The people involved in brewing are generally good guys, so I enjoy the people and I also enjoy creating beers true to style and to the best of my abilities. Seeing people enjoy my beer on Friday night is very satisfying.

What's the inspiration behind Jaipur?
I think the American craft styles are the inspiration. Although I haven't used as much crystal malt as should classically be used. I prefer a lighter, cleaner malt base, which allows the hops to really shine in the flavour.

DAISY CUTTER

Proof of the versatility of the pale ale, Daisy Cutter is dank, aromatic, and quenchingly dry

Half Acre may be an elder statesman in the Chicago brewing scene these days, but when Gabriel Magliaro founded the brewery in 2006, it was one of just a few small upstarts in the Windy City.

Fast-forward, and things have certainly changed around town. As of this summer, there are officially over 70 breweries in Chicago proper, and 115 in the surrounding suburbs. Half Acre may not have worked single-handedly to transform the brewing scene in this Midwestern powerhouse – but its continuing influence can't be denied.

To best appreciate Half Acre, it's worth travelling back to 2009 by way of its flagship Daisy Cutter. One of the first beers that Half Acre produced at its Lincoln Ave brewery, Daisy Cutter was initially developed as a special release bomber. Following a surge in popularity and demand, it was later released in tallboy cans emblazoned with daisies. Nowadays, you're likely to find it in venues scattered all across the Windy City; for many local drinkers, it isn't just Half Acre's best-known brew, but a symbol of Chicago's craft beer scene as a whole.

There are a few reasons why Daisy Cutter captured the imagination when it made its debut. In part, it was developed as a riposte to the hugely hop-led, high-alcohol beers that had dominated the scene. At 5.2%, relatively light of body, and with a lingering, dry finish, it's the kind of quenching pale ale that begs to be glugged after mowing the lawn.

It'll slake your thirst, then, but Daisy Cutter is also a beer of real complexity and elegance. Its aromatic profile veers towards the West Coast, with notes of pine and bright citrus. But it's also dank, bright with peach and mango on the nose, with a lightly sweet, biscuity malt that balances the cumulative bitterness of the hops. That it also pours a vivacious shade of orange – complemented with a pillowy white head – makes it as enjoyable to admire as it is to taste.

the facts

Brewer Half Acre Beer Company
Origin Chicago, Illinois, USA
Strength 5.2%
Type American Pale Ale
Web www.halfacrebeer.com/
Temperature 6-8°C

What's your favourite beer to drink after work?
A Kolsch would probably have to be my bread and butter beer.

Which beer do you wish you'd made?
Schonramer beers are on my desert island list. I would love to spend six months working in, say, a Bavarian wheat beer brewery or a lager brewery to totally master each style. I also love the way Sierra Nevada do things, so brewing there for six months would also be awesome.

Which of your beers best demonstrates who you are as a brewery?
Hard to say, as we do so many different beers. If I had to pick one I would go for Chiron as it's very balanced. Many beers are unbalanced and about making statements rather than something that people want to drink.

SIERRA NEVADA PALE ALE

The classic American Pale Ale that kick-started the trend for increasingly hopped beers and became a landmark on the beer landscape

the facts

Brewer Sierra Nevada
Origin California, United States
Strength 5.6%
Type American Pale Ale
Web www.sierranevada.com
Temperature 6-8°C

The Sierra Nevada story perfectly suits the pursuit of the American Dream. It began with Ken Grossman who opened a home brew supply store in Chico, California, after he travelled through the town and fell in love with it. An avid homebrewer from a young age, Grossman set out to improve his beers and convinced the hop merchants to sell him samples. This was a time when the hop farms primarily sold direct to big brewing companies, and so the 'small bundles' of off-cuts amounted to 50kg (100lb) bales of each hop variety.

It didn't matter. It was enough to launch Grossman's experimental beers and he was soon producing hop-forward beers in his small brewhouse. Though Sierra Nevada Stout was the brewery's first beer, their Pale Ale earned them instant acclaim. Constant demand outstripped supply, causing Sierra Nevada to expand twice since they launched in 1981.

It was Grossman's insistence on consistency that defined Sierra Nevada as a crucial lynchpin in the craft beer movement. They weren't just making good beers, they were always making good beers, beers that people could turn to time and time again when they wanted quality and taste. The ethos remains today, and Sierra Nevada run one of the United States' most well regarded beer research and development laboratories.

Their Sierra Nevada is a world classic, and either started the pale ale revolution or arrived just at the right time, depending on who you listen to. It is dark gold in appearance, hazed by the unfiltered yeast content, and capped with a modest white head. The aroma is understated in its fragrance; it has all the American hallmarks that would be expected from the style – the citrus, hop resin, pine and caramalt – but it's sublimely refined. There's also melon and raisin in there, the melon bringing a fresh, sweet pep to the party. As it warms up, the malt leans forward and grabs the nose with fresh baked biscuits and chunks of toffee.

Caramel and juicy, freshly squeezed watermelon land first on the tongue, the sweet invasion somewhat surprising given that modern takes on the American Pale Ale style tend to be very hop-forward. At cooler temperatures, the midsection is defined by a lemon sherbet fizz which leads into the lingering, lemon and lime rind zest bitter finish. Once the drink warms up a little, a crunchy cookie malt develops and sweetens the deal. Fresh grass notes waft in on occasion; otherwise the freshness is driven by the watermelon flavour right at the core of the Sierra Nevada Pale Ale.

It's hoppy without being intense, malty without being too sweet, and an absolute landmark of the beer landscape that must be visited. Start with Sierra Nevada Pale Ale and everything else will follow.

CANNONBALL

An exceptional British take on a classic US West Coast IPA

the facts

Brewer Magic Rock Brewing
Origin Huddersfield, Yorkshire, UK
Strength 7.4%
Type American IPA
Web www.magicrockbrewing.com
Temperature 5-7°C

Huddersfield's Magic Rock Brewing exploded onto the British craft brewing scene in 2011. Its intensely hop forward, American-influenced beers coupled with a range of solid, traditionally inspired cask ales, rapidly earned the Yorkshire-based brewery a lofty reputation among the beer cognoscenti. Magic Rock was able to expand its production significantly when it moved premises in 2015. Here at its new brewery near Huddersfield's town centre it also opened its popular taproom, where customers can enjoy fresh beer direct from the source.

Out of all Magic Rock's core range of beers the one that has perhaps had the largest impact on its success is Cannonball. This American-style West Coast IPA is heavily inspired by beers such as Ballast Point Sculpin and Stone IPA. Cannonball deftly showcases several US hop varieties including Amarillo, Centennial, Citra, Columbus and Simcoe. The beer is classically West Coast with aromas of pine resin and grapefruit on the nose. The palate is awash with notes of citrus, which are deftly balanced by just a touch of sweetness from the malt before being rounded out by a dry, bitter finish.

Perhaps the most remarkable thing about Cannonball is how well balanced it is – and this can make it a little dangerous. It's incredibly drinkable for a 7.4% beer, with barely a hint of alcohol detectable and each sip becoming even more enjoyable than the last. If you do end up getting stuck into a lengthy session on Cannonball, well, don't say we didn't warn you.

THE BLAZING WORLD

"Danksauce"

THE FACTS
Brewer Modern Times Beer
Origin San Diego, California, USA
Strength 6.8%
Flavour Amber Ale
Web www.moderntimesbeer.com
Temperature 6-8°C

The Blazing World is an early example of utopian science fiction from 1666, depicting a peaceful society without societal divisions. Even for a craft brewery, it's unusually vivid subject matter for a beer name. That said, Modern Times is named after a short-lived utopian community from 1850. In fact, almost all its beers are named after real or fictional attempts at utopias.

The beer version of The Blazing World is part of Modern Times' four-strong core range, each grounded in classic styles but with a twist. In that mold, The Blazing World is ostensibly an amber ale, but injected with the huge hop profile of a Double IPA, using Nelson Sauvin, Simcoe and Mosaic. That probably got your attention, if not, then the can label copy describing it as 'danksauce' probably will.

On paper, it sounds a bit messy, but in practice it's one of the best ways to experience these hops. A pleasing shade of bronze, The Blazing World tricks you into expecting caramel sweetness, but nothing is as it seems. The aroma is dominated by that triple-hop-threat and their bracingly dank, garlicky, allium notes.

Then, as you expect either toffee or pine resin, instead your palate is pummelled with blueberries, tropical fruit salad and grape notes. The real wonder is how it's this lush and potent, yet utterly crushable. Your trip to The Blazing World may not be one from which you wish to return.

ETERNAL

A world-beating Session IPA from Yorkshire

THE FACTS
Brewer Northern Monk Brew Co
Origin Leeds, West Yorkshire, UK
Strength 4.5%
Type Session IPA
Web www.northernmonkbrewco.com
Temperature 6-8°C

Eyebrows were raised when Northern Monk Brew Co scored a medal at the World Beer Cup in 2016 for its Session IPA, Eternal. Could an American-style IPA from an English brewery really outgun something from the USA? Upon reflection, though, it made a lot of sense that this world-beating Session IPA came from Yorkshire – a county where 'session beer' is practically the second language.

Northern Monk Brew Co launched in July 2013. Despite modest beginnings, 'New World' IPA and 'Strannik' Imperial Stout earned plaudits and acclaim. With a fair amount of trademark Yorkshire grit, founder Russell Bisset and head brewer Brian Dickson grew their business and, after acquiring their own premises in central Leeds for their brewery, nothing has held them back. A new NMBCo facility has already been built and opened just down the road from the first.

Eternal reflects both the technical accomplishment of this young brewery and its Leeds roots. For, underneath its all-American fanfare of Simcoe and Centennial hops, Eternal's drinkability rests on a dryness and bitterness that anyone who has lived in Yorkshire will instantly recognise. This just-hazy golden beer has spiky aroma of pink grapefruit, pine and lime, and its light-bodied texture floods the mouth with zesty citrus and a touch of pineapple.

This, however, is a beer whose true brilliance lies in its finish. The soft fruit and citrus pith notes evaporate in a gentle mineral bitterness that, on the one hand, quenches completely, and on the other, leaves you wanting to taste Eternal all over again.

ODELL IPA

A classic American IPA bursting with citrus fruit flavours

When Doug Odell founded the brewery that bares his name along with his wife Wynne and sister Corkie, he drew his inspiration from the traditional real ales he experienced while visiting the UK for the first time. Odell is something of a self-confessed Anglophile, and on subsequent trips has usually begun his trips to England with a visit to his favourite Fuller's pub for a few pints of Chiswick Bitter. Such is his passion for the beers of England that Odell even sends his employees to the UK on a sabbatical once they've completed five years of employment at the brewery.

Although Odell's beers are inspired in part by classic British real ales, they also draw influence from the environment in its immediate vicinity. Just like the Rocky Mountains visible from the brewery itself, Odell's beers are large and pronounced in flavour, but not so imposing as the Rockies themselves.

Odell IPA has long been the anchor that holds the brewery's core range of beers steady. It immediately grabs your attention with a label that depicts a rearing blue elephant on a bright orange background. The beer itself pours a similarly vibrant shade of tangerine and to continue the theme there is also a strong aroma of naval orange zest on the nose, accompanied by honeysuckle and freshly milled grain.

To taste, flavours of orange and grapefruit zest mingle with honey-sweet notes from the malted barley, while the finish is dry and cleansingly bitter. Odell IPA delivers a lot of flavour but above all this beer is balanced – something Doug Odell no doubt learned after drinking pints and pints of British real ale and so sought to add that same quality to the beers his brewery produces.

the facts

Brewer Odell Brewing Company
Origin Fort Collins, Colorado, USA
Strength 7%
Type American IPA
Web www.newbelgium.com
Temperature 6-8°C

GREEN DIAMONDS

Tropical, hazy and bewilderingly drinkable

In a particularly industrial corner of Brooklyn, by the Gowanus Canal, a strange phenomenon occurs several times a month: hundreds of people will line up, sometimes from dawn, occasionally even camping overnight, to purchase the latest canned beers from Other Half Brewing Company's taproom.

Founded by experienced brewer Sam Richardson, former chef Matt Monahan and their business partner Andrew Burman, Other Half has quickly a become a bright light in the fast-growing craft beer scene of New York. Recently, the brewery was voted 10th best in the world by the users of RateBeer, and a new, larger taproom has been opened to help accommodate with their enormous popularity.

The queues for the brewery's beers are not just because of their limited availability – these beers are also seen as leading examples of New England/East Coast IPAs, a style driving huge buzz in craft beer at the moment. Other Half continue to mine this super-hazy, highly hopped style thoroughly, producing new beers every week: whether once-in-a-lifetime recipes or exclusive collaborations, or returning favourites from their extensive catalogue, all in tall cans with dazzling designs.

Green Diamonds is just such a favourite, pairing American Amarillo and Australian Galaxy hops for an explosively tropical palate of pineapple, mango, guava and passion fruit. The beer's deep haze is thanks to natural hop and grain proteins, and the beer's use of Golden Promise malt is evident in its silky mouthfeel and rich, juicy texture.

It truly displays Other Half's hallmark: the ability to pack layers of intense, vibrant hop flavour and aroma into every drop. Despite all this intensity, and alcoholic strength, Green Diamonds will amaze you with its sublime drinkability. Just don't be too surprised if you find yourself in Brooklyn in the near future, waiting in line for some.

the facts

Brewer Other Half Brewing Company
Origin Brooklyn, New York, USA
Strength 9.1%
Type Imperial IPA
Web www.otherhalfbrewing.com
Temperature 6-8°C

NINJA VS. UNICORN

A double IPA that leans heavily on the hops, Ninja Vs. Unicorn is unabashedly unbalanced and beautifully bold

In the world of professional kitchens, it's normal to 'stage' – that is, for trainee chefs to spend short stints in some of the world's top restaurants, learning from and cooking alongside award-winning chefs. That model is less common when it comes to beer, but that didn't stop homebrewers Gerrit Lewis and Beejay Oslon from reaching out to the co-owner of De Struise, Urbain Coutteau, with an offer to work for free.

Coutteau took them up on the offer, and the two headed to Oostvleteren, Belgium in 2009, where they got a first-hand experience of the inner workings of a successful brewery. Upon returning to Chicago, they established Pipeworks Brewing Company in 2012. Fast-forward to five years later: in 2017, even in the midst of a fast-growing and highly competitive local beer scene, Pipeworks remains one of the Windy City's standout breweries.

The closest thing Pipeworks has to a flagship beer is its fabulously named Ninja Vs. Unicorn. A bombastic 8% double IPA that's brewed with five pounds of hops per barrel, Ninja Vs. Unicorn was first sold in bombers, which Chicago's craft beer set would trek across the city to score. These days, it retails in vibrant tallboy cans that depict a standoff between a masked ninja and a rainbow-horned unicorn.

One of the frequent insults that critics lob towards double IPAs like Ninja Vs. Unicorn is that they're unbalanced, and in this case, that's certainly true: the beer's malt base is almost undetectable amidst a barrage of intense hop flavours. But this beer was also never intended to demonstrate level-headed equity among its constituent parts. As an unabashed showcase of everything that hops can do, it's explosively flavourful, bright with tangerine notes, as well as pineapple, melon, and mango, all tempered with a dash of piney resin. For hop lovers, this is a sensory feast of a beer.

the facts

Brewer Pipeworks Brewing Company
Origin Chicago, Illinois, USA
Strength 8%
Type Double IPA
Web www.pdubs.net/
Temperature 6-8°C

PLINY THE ELDER

Immaculate flavours of citrus and pine combine in one of the world's greatest beers

When Russian River Brewing Company co-founder and brewer Vinnie Cilurzo first brewed a Double IPA called Pliny the Elder in the year 2000, it's unlikely he realised that the brewery had just created what would become a cult success. Cilurzo had been brewing Double IPA at the Blind Pig Brewpub in Santa Rosa, California as far back as 1994, before he and his wife and business partner Natalie founded Russian River in 1997. However, Pliny – as it has affectionately come to be known – would be the beer that would earn them international renown.

Pliny is named after the Roman botanist, Pliny the Elder, who lived between 23 to 79 CE before meeting his demise in Pompeii, during the infamous eruption of Vesuvius. Before his untimely death, Pliny wrote of a plant he called Lupus Salictarius – now better known as Humulus Lupulus – or hops. Pliny the beer is a homage to hops and uses the Amarillo, Centennial, CTZ and Simcoe varieties in gratuitous quantities to deliver the pungent aromatics and resinous body that this beer has built its reputation on.

Perhaps the real beauty of Pliny the Elder is just how easy it is to drink for an 8% beer. Its classically West Coast in appearance and flavour, pouring the colour of bright cold and releasing aromas of pine sap and pink grapefruit as you do so. Those aromas translate beautifully onto the palate, with a little bready malt also getting into the mix before the resinous, bitter finish leaves your mouth puckering for another sip. If you can find it, and California is the best place to do this, then Pliny is best drunk as fresh as possible to enjoy those delicious hop oils at their best.

the facts

Brewer Russian River Brewing Company
Origin Santa Rosa, California, USA
Strength 8%
Type Double IPA
Web www.russianriverbrewing.com
Temperature 8-10°C

ENJOY BY IPA

This outstanding Double IPA will self-destruct

A major challenge for craft breweries has been educating consumers and retailers about the importance of freshness. The gorgeous aromatics and flavours found in IPAs are derived from hop oils and compounds which deteriorate quickly. One way to help convey the importance of freshness to people is to give prominence to packing dates and best before dates on labelling. Some, like Stone Brewing, take this even further.

Enjoy By IPA is a Double IPA with its best before date printed large on the front of the label. In fact, its BBD is technically part of the beer's name. What's even more impressive is that Stone's Enjoy By IPA is given a shelf life of just 37 days to be consumed from the moment the bottles are filled. By way of comparison, most heavily hopped beers from even the most fastidious brewers will be given at least 90-120 days' shelf life.

In typical Stone Brewing style, almost everything about this beer is over the top. For starters, it's even stronger than their core range Double IPA 'Ruination'. It is also hopped with a staggering 12 different varieties from around the world: Ahtanum, Super Galena, Simcoe, Delta, Target, Amarillo, Calypso, Cascade, Galaxy, Nelson Sauvin, Motueka and Helga. If that wasn't enough, it's typically sold in 650ml (22oz) bottles (although it has also been sold in 330ml cans).

Its heady strength is masked by the sheer oiliness and fruitiness of its hop character. The resinous aroma of pine, stone fruit and grapefruit gives you a fair idea of what you'll taste, but this beer is served so fresh that the hops practically glide across your palate, all while your brain is telling you that you've just bitten into an overripe peach. It might be a challenge to drink it fresh enough, but it's certainly not a challenge to enjoy.

the facts

Brewer Stone Brewing
Origin Escondido, California, USA
Strength 9.4%
Type Double IPA
Web www.stonebrewing.com
Temperature 6-8°C

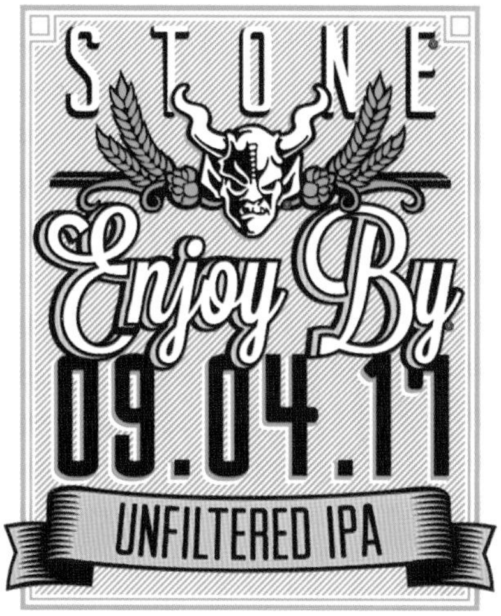

HEADY TOPPER

A hazy, iconic, and much-imitated standard-bearer of New England brewing

It would be difficult to overstate the influence and importance of Heady Topper, both in its native New England brewing scene, in the US generally, and even within the global beer community.

Packaged in distinctive silver cans that feature a whimsical, moustachioed gent supping a pint, a cloud of whole-cone hops bursting from his head, the unfiltered double IPA has inspired countless imitations. It also helped put Vermont on the map as a new brewing capital. Fourteen years after The Alchemist kegged the first iterations of Heady for its (now-shuttered) brewpub, and six years after the DIPA made its debut in cans, it's as coveted and sought-after as ever.

Part of the fervour comes down to simple supply-and-demand economics. Brewed at The Alchemist's location in Waterbury (the brewery also runs a second production facility and visitor centre in nearby Stowe, Vermont, where the exceptional Focal Banger IPA is made), Heady Topper is formally distributed within a 25-mile radius of where it's made. To get hold of a four-pack of cans either requires a Vermont road trip or some well-connected trading partners.

Those who've never had the pleasure of sipping Heady straight from the can (as its all-caps instructions demand) might wonder if this infamous beer really merits the relentless adulation, never mind the best-in-the-world distinctions.

It's true that Heady may have less of a profound impact on seasoned IPA drinkers these days; its once ground-breaking haze, reliance on bold aroma hops, use of dry hopping, and beguiling dankness have become the new standard. But its vividness, its tropicality, and softness on the palate still make it tremendously difficult to outclass.

While Heady Topper's flavour profile is neon-bright, it's also profoundly elegant. In the narrative of a single sip, its flavour pirouettes from tangerine to floral notes, from mango to a subtle earthiness, finishing with a gentle but lingering bitterness. The sensation is almost culinary, akin to having savoured a perfectly composed tasting menu.

the facts

Brewer The Alchemist
Origin Waterbury, Vermont, USA
Strength 8%
Type Double IPA
Web www.alchemistbeer.com/
Temperature 6-8°C

ALL DAY IPA

More refreshing than water, and so sharp you could cut yourself when drinking it

A number of breweries, particularly in the US and UK, seem obsessed with making bigger and bolder IPAs, chucking whole hop bales into the kettle to make them as aggressively hoppy as possible. The results are interesting, and a lot of flavour comes out of some of the better Big IPA beers, but nine times out of ten they set fire to your tongue and melt your eyeballs in the process.

In this great race to the top of Hop Mountain, one brewery has opted to stand still. It's a relief to see Founders taking the novel approach of keeping the strength at a reasonable 4.7% ABV for their All Day IPA, which it bills as a 'session beer'.

It pours a sparkling bright, pale copper coloured beer with very little head retention. The aroma is full and fresh with juicy tropical pineapple and mango notes, sweet fruit juice and honey. The body is brilliant in its crisp sharpness, a stark contrast to many US IPAs which can be quite thick and cloying from the buckets of caramalt they use to balance the buckets of hops.

Grapefruit is a common aroma and flavour derived from US hops and it usually plays a supporting role within the larger citrus fruit chorus, but in All Day IPA it stands front and centre and sings its heart out. For a moment there's the sudden belief that this actually is freshly squeezed grapefruit juice, then lemongrass, lime zest and passing hints of malt step up and take the flavour toward the quick, clean finish.

It's the finish that nails All Day IPA as a session beer, along with the uncomplicated, razor sharp taste that cuts through thirst, food and post-work mental cobwebs. Brilliantly, it's also available in cans, so chuck the cloudy lemonade away and take this on picnics instead.

the facts

Brewer Founders
Origin Michigan, USA
Strength 4.7%
Type IPA
Web www.foundersbrewing.com
Temperature 4-8°C

HOPHANDS

A juicy, cloudy, hop-led flagship beer by the darlings of the East Coast brewing scene

THE FACTS
Brewer Tired Hands Brewing Company
Origin Ardmore, Pennsylvania, USA
Strength 5.5%
Type American Pale Ale
Web www.tiredhands.com/
Temperature 6-8°C

Well before Tired Hands comes into view, you'll notice the crowd. A member of a coterie of East Coast breweries that represent craft beer's 2017 zeitgeist, Tired Hands is infamous for the hundreds-deep queues that snake from its Fermentaria location through the parking lots and back-alleys of Ardmore.

If you want to guarantee you'll walk away with several four-packs of whatever limited-edition release the brewery is slinging, steel yourself for several hours spent outdoors.

Jean Broillet IV launched Tired Hands' Brew Café in 2012. In lieu of a core range, his yen for experimentation saw the brewery release a variety of surprising, adjunct-laden beers, of which its Milkshake IPA series is a famous (and coveted) example.

HopHands is the brewery's flagship pale ale. It's also relatively easy to get your hands on, especially since the brewery's General Store opened this past summer. At first blush, HopHands might seem almost pedestrian by Tired Hands' standards: no fruit extracts, no lactose. Instead, it's hopped with Simcoe, Centennial, and Amarillo, which lends it a 'crushable' juiciness, as well as notes of nectarine, kiwi, and a moreish dankness. Perhaps the most typically Tired Hands flourish is the fact it's brewed with oats, which impart a cloudy appearance that has become something like the brewery's signature.

AXE EDGE

This English gentleman-thug will rough you up and buy you a pint afterwards

THE FACTS
Brewer Buxton Brewery
Origin Buxton, UK
Strength 6.8%
Type IPA
Web www.buxtonbrewery.co.uk
Temperature 6-8°C

Buxton Brewery is another example of a quickly expanding start-up brewery. Their range of big, bold beers, from Russian Imperial Stouts to Imperial Smoked Rye Porters, quickly caught the attention of the craft beer world.

Axe Edge is their Double IPA. The aroma is a mellow blend of almost everything the hop world can give us; from the New World tropicality of pineapple, mango and lychee; America's orange, grapefruit and pine, to the floral meadows and freshly cut grass fields of England. It's divine: a tranquil harmony of blended aromas that lulls you into a false sense of security for the taste to come.

That first mouthful of this beer is when the name is suddenly appreciated. The sweetness of rich, juicy lychee, passion fruit, orange and pineapple is shattered by a sudden strike of resinous hops carried by a boozy edge. A distinctive, toffee malt flavour is all too brief before a highly bitter, citrus sharp finish sweeps in. That finish is also very dry, so avoid naked flames or you may catch alight.

Axe Edge is not something that can be drunk in large quantities, but it's a key example of when breweries hop a beer to high heaven and get it right. If you have time for only one beer and want to make it count, or you're flagging during an all day session, Axe Edge will sort you out a treat.

JULIUS

A modern classic, this East Coast IPA bursts with juicy mango, orange, and other fruit-led hop flavours

According to Tree House's co-founder Nate Lanier, Julius – the brewery's hugely acclaimed flagship IPA – is a 'fluffy' beer. Or, to use more common parlance, it's beautifully soft on the palate, absent any hop astringency, biting bitterness, or other rough-around-the-edges attributes that would interrupt its silky drinking experience.

That delectable consistency is what Lanier believes makes Julius – which has been described in beer circles as one of the best IPAs in existence today – such a standout. That and its juicy-fruit hop character. Lanier claims that the beer's recipe was inspired by packets of dried mango slices, and it's true that Julius is as fruit-forward as a morning smoothie. A beautiful orange hue in the glass, it's also ripe with flavours of freshly squeezed tangerine – even its name is reference to its juiciness (in the States, an Orange Julius is a milkshake-like drink made with orange, milk, sugar, and vanilla).

Alongside brews made by East Coast peers like Tired Hands, The Alchemist, and Trillium, Tree House's IPAs aren't just delicious: they represent the latest evolution of the style. These IPAs trade in softness, in bold fruit flavours, in low bitterness, and in a rich, cloudy haze; like Julius, many look much more like juice than like beer.

Consumers can't get enough of this style; Julius's apricot-hued cans are traded and shared with huge amounts of fervour. In response to its soaring popularity, the brewery is in the midst of constructing a colossal new facility in nearby Charlton, Massachusetts – an $18.5 million project that will be capable of turning out 150,000 barrels per year.

It's a dramatic upgrade for Tree House – especially considering that the brewery was established in a small barn just five years ago. And its good news for fans of the brewery who, up until this point, have had to drive into remote Western Mass – and queue for hours at a time – to get their hands on these most coveted of cans.

the facts

Brewer Tree House Brewing Company
Origin Monson, Massachusetts, USA
Strength 6.8%
Type American IPA
Web www.treehousebrew.com
Temperature 6-8°C

WHITE IPA

Pivovar Raven, Pilsen, Czech Republic
Type White IPA Strength 6.3%

• The Czech town of Pilsen is known around the world for being the home of Pilsner Urquell. However, even this relatively quiet Czech town hasn't been able to resist the lure of modern styles. Pivovar Raven crafts beers that reflect both modern culture and the traditional heritage of the town, with this citrus forward IPA brewed with the familiar, dry and mineral finish this town's well water is famous for.

SWAMI'S IPA

Pizza Port Brewing Company, San Diego, California, USA
Type American IPA Strength 6.8%

• Pizza Port Brewing Company has numerous Southern California locations, each its own brewpub crafting its own beers. However our favourite has to be the Ocean Beach location in San Diego. Here you can wile away an evening chowing down on great pizza, playing a few arcade games and enjoying beers like Swami's IPA, a classically West Coast, citrus forward IPA.

NANBAN KANPAI

Pressure Drop, London, UK
Type Fruit IPA Strength 6.5%

• Brewed in collaboration with Masterchef winner Tim Anderson, and a staple on the menu at his Japanese restaurant Nanban, this IPA gets a boost from additions of orange, grapefruit and yuzu juice. Whilst delicious on its own, bursting with citrus acidity and hoppy bite, it really shines when paired with any oily fish or the richer, spicier flavours on Nanban's menu.

TRINITY

Redemption, London, UK
Type Pale Ale Strength 3%

• It's unknown exactly what kind of witchcraft Tottenham's Redemption Brewery use to cram so much body and flavour into its 3% Trinity but whatever it is they use it to great effect. Aromas of lemon peel and candied orange translate beautifully onto the palate, which is supported by a lovely digestive biscuit flavoured malt body. Trinity is a beer that can be enjoyed all day long.

XS IMPERIAL IPA

Saltaire Brewery, Saltaire, UK
Type Double IPA Strength 9.5%

• The UK's modern breweries are doing an incredible job of producing hop bombs that rival the best being produced in the US. One of the best examples is, as is often the case, not talked about enough. Saltaire's XS Imperial IPA is awash with the resinous, piney character of Simcoe and the intensely juicy, stone fruit quality of Galaxy, all wrapped up with a clean malt base. Those who know, know.

HOP CANDY

Siren Craft Brew, Finchampstead, UK
Type Double IPA Strength 9.2%

• In the fast-moving world of beer trends, the release of Siren Craft Beer's firmly West Coast Hop Candy amid the craze for East Coast IPAs seemed to be slightly strange timing, but this dazzling double IPA and its fans didn't seem to care. A potent aroma of pine sap and lime gets your attention, before spoiling you with a tropical palate of mango and passion fruit.

PUFF

Sixpoint Brewery, Brooklyn, New York, USA
Type Double IPA Strength 9.8%

• Described by the brewery as a hazier, gnarlier take on the flagship Resin DIPA, Puff is both an acknowledgement of the beer's cloudy appearance as well as its unabashed dankness. Double dry-hopped with Citra and Mosaic, this potent brew shares some of the attributes of a classic New England-style IPA, though it's significantly more bitter, bracing, and piney on the palate.

THE PUPIL

Societe Brewing Company, California, USA
Type American IPA Strength 7.5%

• With its accomplished array of beers from IPAs, to stouts to complex Belgian styles, Societe quickly asserted its credentials in the brewing Mecca of San Diego. The Pupil is an IPA in the modern style, eschewing crystal malt and intense bitterness, instead focusing on soft, tropical fruit flavours over a soft and pillowy pale malt backbone. The gentle bitterness will soon have you wanting another sip.

WHITE SHIELD

A characterful, beautiful, multi award-winning beer with enough marmalade to keep Paddington happy

White Shield is a legendary beer, even in recent history. It is still brewed at the White Shield Brewery in Burton-on-Trent, beside the massive plant of its brand owner, Molson Coors. Its corporate owner is keen to retain the brand's identity and reputation, keeping head brewer Steve Wellington on site to steward the brand back to its best, after decades of being brewed elsewhere. It is the most awarded bottled ale in the history of CAMRA beer festivals, and deserves every single accolade.

A deep, orangey amber, White Shield looks a little like a glass of smooth marmalade, something definitely present in both its aroma and taste. The beer is bottle-conditioned, making for a very lively and foamy pour. Do so with care if you want to avoid the conditioning yeast entering the glass, though it certainly doesn't do any harm to the beer's flavour. If the yeast is left out, the beer absolutely shines: rich, bright and warming to look at.

There is a slightly grassy, floral edge to its spiced orange and fruitcake aroma. It's a heady, slightly boozy nose but rich with marmalade, a little ginger and caramelising sugar. The high carbonation makes a beer that is sharp, peppery and sparkling with rich, orangey sweetness. After generous helpings of marmalade and treacle, White Shield delivers a full-bodied, feet-planted, hips-twisting, straight-arm punch to the bitter section of the palate that knocks you about two hundred years back in time. The finish is peppery, floral and unforgivingly dry.

You can't dislike the aggressive yet well-meaning boisterousness of this as-it-was IPA. It's the sort of broad-shouldered, loveable old chap at the bar who looks stronger than you'll ever be, slaps you on the back hard enough to burst a lung and tells you to drink up. It's not the strongest or the hoppiest IPA in the world, or even in this publication, but it might be the one with the biggest character.

the facts

Brewer Molson Coors
Origin Burton-upon-Trent, UK
Strength 5.6%
Type English IPA
Web www.molsoncoors.com
Temperature 9-12°C

THE BEER TALKING

STEFANO COSSI
MOLSON COORS

What do you most enjoy about brewing?
The brewing process allows constant improvement and development to refine the beers and make them the best they can be. It is very rewarding when someone enjoys the beers that you make – however the worst critics are the brewers themselves!

What's the inspiration behind White Shield?
White Shield is inspired by Burton's success as a UK beer town during the 19th century when leading Burton breweries developed IPAs. I am fascinated by Britain's brewing heritage and in my current role I have the chance to emphasise the use of traditional techniques.

Which of your beers best demonstrates who you are?
It has to be White Shield, an iconic beer which I am proud to brew.

SHAPE SHIFTER IPA

Fourpure Brewing Co, London, UK

Type American IPA Strength 6.4%

Whilst Fourpure's core range shoots for inclusivity over eccentricity, its Adventure Series features more, well, adventurous beers like Shape Shifter IPA, hopped with Mosaic, Centennial and Citra. There are resinous, herbal edges to its aroma of mango and pine, whilst waves of tropical fruit and oily hop bitterness wash across the palate. A balance of intensity and clarity that impresses brewers.

INTERURBAN IPA

Fremont Brewing, Seattle, Washington, USA

Type American IPA Strength 6.2%

Chinook, Centennial and Amarillo hops combine in this classically Northwestern IPA from one of Seattle's finest breweries, Fremont. The nose is initially marijuana-dank but is underpinned by juicy fragrances of naval orange. On the palate are flavours of grapefruit, honey-sweetness from the malt and the bitter tang of pine resin, which leads to a bitter and resinous finish.

WEST COAST IPA

Green Flash Brewing Co., San Diego, California, USA

Type Double IPA Strength 8.1%

Green Flash's West Coast IPA sparked a sea change when it was first released back in 2005: not only did it help kick off the concept of the 'West Coast IPA', but it also changed the way consumers approached hoppy beers. Following a recipe rejig in 2014, the puckering, resinous beer (technically a Double IPA, at 8.1% ABV) now features Citra alongside the original hop bill of Simcoe, Columbus, Centennial, and Cascade.

60 MINUTE IPA

Dogfish Head, Delaware, USA

Type IPA Strength 6%

60 Minute IPA is boiled for 60 minutes, with hops being continuously added throughout the process, rather than in bulk batches at specific points as almost all other brewers do. It creates a 6% ABV beer boasting 60 IBUs. There's also a 90 and 120 Minute IPA in the range, with the 60 Minute being the lightest in body but highest in hop aroma and dry, bittering flavour.

RALPHIUS

Free Will Brewing Co., Pennsylvania, USA

Type Russian Imperial Stout Strength 15.3%

Free Will's Ralphius is a tour de force of a stout. A year spent ageing in bourbon barrels gives this brew monumental heft, as well as complexity: beyond the expected flavour notes of chocolate, roasty coffee, and vanilla, it's also imbued with a rich jamminess, a touch of piquant aniseed, and caramelised molasses. A truly exceptional example of the style.

PROJECT HAZE 002

Funk Brewing Company, Pennsylvania, USA

Type Double IPA Strength 7.6%

Though the brewery's name might suggest an infatuation with wild yeast, Funk is best known for its queue-worthy IPAs (and that moniker actually originates with brewer and co-founder Kyle Funk). When it was released in autumn of 2016, this brew certainly attracted crowds. With the appearance of melted ice cream, the aroma of Um Bongo, and the flavour of a fruit smoothie, Funk's Project Haze 002 is East Coast-style DIPA perfection.

LAMBO DOOR

Grimm Artisanal Ales, Brooklyn, New York, USA

Type Double IPA Strength 8%

Husband-and-wife team Joe and Lauren Grimm are nomadic brewers who develop recipes in their Brooklyn apartment before crafting their products at friends' breweries. That their IPAs and Double IPAs are some of the most coveted in the country speaks to their talent. Lambo Door – described as 'Gummi Bear juice' – is a delectable dessert of a DIPA, with soft carbonation, a rich mouthfeel, and juicy fruit hop flavours.

DOUBLE GALAXY

Hill Farmstead, Greensboro, Vermont, USA

Type Double IPA Strength 7.8%

When the brewing acumen of Shaun Hill and Australian Galaxy hops combine the results are as spectacular as you might expect. This is a soft, juicy and hazy IPA in the New England style, bursting with opal fruit sticky sweetness and juicy notes of peach and apricot. There's barely a hint of bitterness as the beer seems to delicately evaporate off your palate.

STAY G-O-L-D

Interboro Spirits & Ales, Brooklyn, New York, USA
Type IPA Strength 6%

Demonstrating the overlap between craft beer and other subcultures, Interboro's brewmaster became a friend of hip-hop duo Run The Jewels through his previous job at a record label. This eventually resulted in a collaboration: Stay G-O-L-D, after the RTJ song of the same name. A super-juicy IPA using Mosaic hop dust, it's bursting with dank, tropical notes and smooth citrus flavours.

FLOWER POWER

Ithaca Beer Co., Ithaca, New York, USA
Type American IPA Strength 7.5%

Well before the Northeast became the brewing powerhouse it is today, there was Ithaca. When the brewery released Flower Power in 2004, it was one of the first breweries to bring pungent and intense West Coast-style IPAs to the East Coast. Though tastes have evolved, this legendary IPA – which, as its name suggests, is bountifully floral, as well as rich in tropical fruit flavours – remains a classic deserving of acclaim.

RUSTBUCKET

Kinnegar Brewing, Co Donegal, Ireland
Type Rye Ale Strength 5.1%

County Donegal's Kinnegar Brewing have a knack for brewing well-rounded, harmonious beers, regardless of style or strength. The gentle spiciness of rye is just one element to this moreish amber beer, which also neatly stacks spiced orange hop notes and clean bitterness atop a foundation texture of biscuit-like sweetness. An uncomplicated and beautifully composed beer with broad appeal.

MOOIE NEL IPA

Jopen, Haarlem, The Netherlands
Type American IPA Strength 6.5%

If you ever find yourself in The Netherlands then do yourself a favour and make a beeline to the town of Haarlem and to Jopen brewery. Here you can relax in quaint surroundings and watch the world go about its business while you enjoy beers such as Mooie Nel. An IPA in the American style, Mooie Nel packs in familiar flavours of grapefruit zest, candied orange that lead to a subtly bittersweet finish.

TASTY JUICE

Lervig Aktiebryggeri, Stavanger, Norway
Type American IPA Strength 6%

It looks like pink grapefruit juice, but rest assured that this IPA is an entirely different kind of juice. One made with a double dose of Citra hops, which supplies a fruit-punch cornucopia of flavours (mango, pineapple, passion fruit). But in addition to its fruit-forward reputation, Citra also has a savoury, pungent edge, which is just the quality needed to lend this IPA some depth.

SIP OF SUNSHINE

Lawson's Finest Liquids, Warren, Vermont, USA
Type Imperial IPA Strength 8%

Whilst easily as influential as some of its more famous neighbours, Lawson's Sip of Sunshine stands apart. Its high ABV is masked completely, both by its zesty, floral aroma and the sharp, sugary notes of pineapple, orange and lime on the palate. Bitterness is slightly more present than in some of its peers, but this only helps to balance its juicy intensity.

LIL' SUMPIN' SUMPIN' ALE

Lagunitas Brewing Company, Petaluma, California, USA
Type American Wheat Strength 7.5%

Lil' Sumpin' Sumpin' Ale might be a precursor to East Coast IPA, taking a rich, silky malt base boosted by wheat and integrating a juicy, tropical fruit hop character. Despite the high ABV and supercharged body, pineapple, kiwi and orange notes shine in this cleverly constructed, filtered wheat beer/IPA hybrid.

DINNER

Maine Beer Company, Freeport, Maine, USA
Type Double IPA Strength 8.2%

Maine Beer Co encourages customers to drink this much-heralded Double IPA on the same day it's bought, and it's true that this phenomenal beer, when fresh, offers a master-class in the style. Described as one of the best DIPAs currently being made in the US, Dinner is supremely elegant and balanced – its caramel malt profile and tropical hopping co-exist in perfect harmony.

SIMCOE

Mallinson's Brewing Company, Huddersfield, UK

Type Pale Ale Strength 3.9%

• If you want to learn about the variances in flavour between different hop varieties then delve into the single hop series from Yorkshire's Mallinson's Brewing Company. Each of these single hopped beers excels in its own way but a highlight is the one that showcases Simcoe. Lingering notes of mango flesh and pine resin combine in this delicately floral beer, which excels on cask and in bottle.

FOGGIER WINDOW

Monkish Brewing Co., Los Angeles, USA

Type Double IPA Strength 8.1%

• The name gives a good indication of this hyped beer's turbidity: resembling a mixture of milk and orange juice (or, less charitably, a glass of butterscotch pudding), Foggier Window is all about the haze. But even the murk-shy should be convinced after a sip. A double dry-hopped take on the brewery's Foggy Window DIPA, Foggier Window is made with Citra, Nelson Sauvin, and Galaxy, meaning it falls squarely in the beery zeitgeist.

2X4

Melvin Brewing, Jackson Hole, Wyoming, USA

Type Double IPA Strength 10%

• Once described as "the best thing to ever come out of Wyoming," Melvin Brewing quickly established itself as one of the finest producers of modern hoppy beer when it launched in 2009. One of the beers that put it on the map was 2x4, a riotously hop forward double IPA, showcasing the Columbus, Centennial, Citra and Simcoe varieties and is loaded with intense flavours of citrus and tropical fruit, as you'd expect.

CARTE BLANCHE

Breakside Brewery, Portland, Oregon, USA

Type Wild Ale Strength 7.7%

• While barrel ageing is an increasingly common practice in the world of craft beer, the use of gin barrels remains rare (most gin doesn't spend time on oak, after all). But in Carte Blanche, one of Breakside Brewery's experimental 'b-sides', gin makes a compelling addition to this lightly tart wild ale, bringing with it a perfume of herbaceous botanicals, vanilla, and citrus to round out the Brettanomyces pungency.

DOBBER

Marble Beer, Manchester, UK

Type IPA Strength 6.5%

• This once discontinued beer was recently revived thanks to the efforts of beer writer Matthew Curtis (you can thank me later) and was restored to its rightful place in Marble Beer's core lineup. Citra, Mosaic, Azzaca and Nelson Sauvin combine to wonderful effect to produce spritzy flavours of mango and lime zest, which are delicately underpinned by a biscuit malt character.

CITY OF THE SUN

Modern Times Beer, San Diego, California, USA

Type American IPA Strength 7.6%

• In this release, hops are at the fore – so much so that the brewery describes malt as being 'barely detectable'. Those who appreciate balance may quail at this beer, but for lovers of new world hops like Mosaic and Motueka, City of the Sun is a decadent feast for the senses. Sticky, resinous, tropical, and citric, it's a perfectly contemporary take on the West Coast IPA.

SCULPIN IPA

Ballast Point, San Diego, California, USA

Type IPA Strength 7%

• Ballast Point's strong-yet-smooth, amber-coloured IPA is brimming with scents of mango, grapefruit, a little spice and syrup. Sculpin's flavour is supremely balanced, even-handed in its dispensing of rich, fruity sweetness and pithy, dry bitterness, until it reaches a generous finish of melon, honey and mango, sharpened by alcohol and spice.

HOPPINESS

Moor Beer Company, Bristol, UK

Type IPA Strength 6.5%

• Sitting comfortably in the territory that lies between a traditional English and modern American IPA is Hoppiness from Bristol's Moor Beer Company. There's plenty of malt backbone here, evoking flavours of burnt sugar and toffee. These are contrasted by a bold hop profile, showcasing flavours of guava and mango before petering out with a bitter, grassy finish.

WHIRLPOOL

Night Shift Brewing, Everett, Massachusetts, USA
Type American Pale Ale Strength 4.5%

• In a brewery, the whirlpool is where hops can be added to extract flavour and aroma, without adding much bitterness. It's an apt title for Night Shift's pale ale, which has a gorgeous, hazy golden colour and a sessionable, light body. Peach, kiwi and lime aromas burst from the head, whilst the soft, citrusy palate makes the first glass all too quick.

SNAKES ALIVE

One Mile End, London, UK
Type Double IPA Strength 8%

• Although it now brews at its production brewery in Tottenham, North London, One Mile End started out at the East End address from which it took its name. Snakes Alive is a tropically tasty DIPA, brewed in the modern American style. Expect plenty of juicy hop notes in the form of kumquat and lychee before a little bit of lemon zest tinged bitterness comes in at the finish.

AMAZING HAZE

Stigbergets Bryggeri, Gothenburg, Sweden
Type American IPA Strength 6.5%

• Leave it to the brewers at Stigbergets to take a style of beer most associated with the East Coast of the US and to do an exceptional iteration of it some 3,500 miles away. Amazing Haze looks sludgy but is highly slurpable, and – thanks to a double dry hopping of Mosaic – is as sweet, fruit forward, and irresistible as a tropical smoothie straight out of the blender.

LONG WHITE CLOUD

Tempest Brewing Co., Tweedbank, UK
Type New Zealand Pale Ale Strength 5.6%

• Referencing the translation of the Maori name for New Zealand, Scottish brewery Tempest brews Long White Cloud as its flagship Extra Pale Ale. Very pale gold in colour, this beer has a very gentle grain character, while New Zealand hop varieties add rounded, vinous and grape-like fruit notes. Pithy lemon and lime flavours contribute to the clean bitterness of its dry finish.

HOUBLON CHOUFFE

Brasserie d'Achouffe, Achouffe Belgium
Type IPA Strength 9%

• Houblon Chouffe was released in 2006 after the brewers visited the US. The beer is the brainchild of that visit, a union of brash American IPA and subtle Belgian triple style ales. It delivers the resinous pine and citrus boom of American IPA rounded by fruity, spicy Belgian yeast esters, all wrapped up in a light, hazy gold package.

GO TO IPA

Stone Brewing, California, USA & Berlin, Germany
Type Session IPA Strength 4.5%

• The trend for lower-strength but highly-hopped 'Session IPA' has been fully embraced by hopheads that don't like their night to end too early. Stone's Go To IPA ticks all the boxes for this style, and gets its hop additions as late (and as big) as possible to deliver a full West Coast hop character of citrus and pine without being overpoweringly bitter.

TODD THE AXE MAN

Surly Brewing Company, Minnesota, USA
Type American IPA Strength 6.5%

• Minnesota's Surly Brewing Co collaborated on this beer with Denmark's Amager Brewery and named it after the then Surly Brewmaster (now at 3 Floyds) Todd Haug. This impressive riff on an American West Coast IPA uses English Golden Promise malt to provide a solid platform for US Citra and Mosaic hops, bringing forth modern, juicy flavours of mango, lychee and pink grapefruit.

"THIS IMPRESSIVE RIFF ON AN AMERICAN WEST COAST IPA BRINGS FORTH MANGO, LYCHEE AND PINK GRAPEFRUIT FLAVOURS"

FOCAL BANGER

The Alchemist, Stowe, Vermont, USA

Type American IPA Strength 7%

• The Alchemist may be better known for its double IPA, Heady Topper, but that's not the only intensely hoppy and aromatic IPA this brewery produces. Focal Banger is a modern IPA packed with Mosaic and Citra Hop Varieties. It begins with a nose full of dank citrus and tropical fruit aromas, leading to a savoury finish that will have you thinking of garlic and chives.

CRUCIAL TAUNT

The Veil Brewing Co., Richmond, Virginia, USA

Type Double IPA Strength 8%

• Virginia's The Veil Brewing Co. has rapidly asserted itself as one of the masters of the modern, hazy and juicy American double IPA. Its recipes are ever changing, seemingly altering with the brewer's current state of mind. Crucial Taunt is but one of many highlights featuring zingy hop notes of peach and apricot with a hint of tingling citrus bitterness in the finish.

ARE WE THERE YET?

Threes Brewing and Evil Twin Brewing, Brooklyn, NY and Copenhagen, Denmark

Type Triple IPA Strength 10.3%

• A triple IPA that's triple dry-hopped, Threes Brewing's collaboration with Evil Twin, Are We There Yet?, is one memorable beer. A luscious blend of Galaxy, Citra and Mosaic hops, as well as Citra Lupulin Powder, goes into this exceptional beer. Juicy with soft notes of strawberry, orange, mango, and peach, its smoothness belies its strength – and it's evidence of Threes Brewing's rising-star status.

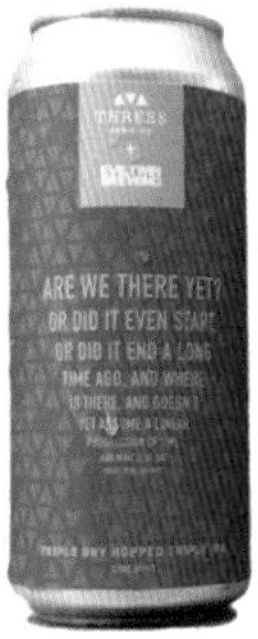

SUPERCHARGER APA

Panhead Custom Ales, Upper Hutt, New Zealand

Type American Pale Ale Strength 5.7%

• Despite only being founded as recently as 2013, Panhead have quickly become one of the most awarded breweries in New Zealand. Somewhat controversially they sold to the Lion Group of breweries in 2017, although the beer tastes as good as ever. Supercharger is classically American in profile, with a spun sugar sweetness carrying forth waves of grapefruit pith tinged bitterness.

PSEUDOSUE

Toppling Goliath Brewing Co., Iowa, USA

Type American Pale Ale Strength 5.8%

• Named in honour of Sue – the 67 million-year-old T. Rex fossil that's located in Chicago's Field Museum – PseudoSue cans come proudly emblazoned with T. Rex imagery. But this 5.8% APA is more delicious than fearsome. Single-hopped with Citra, it's a perfect showcase for the hop's notes of mango, citrus, and other tropical fruits. Delicately balanced and gently bitter, it's a superbly drinkable brew.

SONOMA

Track Brewing Co., Manchester, UK

Type Pale Ale Strength 3.8%

• Sonoma, from Manchester's Track Brewing Co. takes its name from the valley in California that's home to breweries that have inspired this hoppy pale ale, such as Russian River. Track Brewing takes familiar Northern American hop flavours such as mango, citrus and pine nut and wraps them up in a satisfyingly bitter, low alcohol, sessionable package that is quintessentially Mancunian in style.

DIALED-IN

Trillium Brewing Company, Massachusetts, USA

Type Double IPA Strength 8.5%

• With its Dialed-In series of double IPAs Trillium has taken its signature soft and juicy IPA blueprint and given it a twist by adding grape juice mid fermentation to complement the hops. Imagine Nelson Sauvin hops mingling with fresh Sauvignon Blanc juice and you'll understand why it's so sought-after.

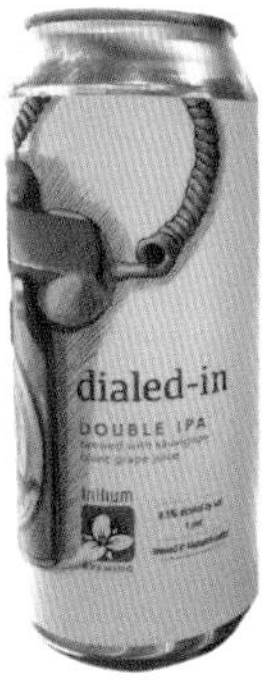

NUGGET NECTAR

Tröegs Independent Brewing, Hershey, Pennsylvania, USA

Type Imperial Amber Ale Strength 7.5%

• Tröegs's Nugget Nectar is released every January. Made with Nugget, Palisade, Simcoe, Tomahawk, and Warrior hops, it's a sticky, resinous, highly bitter brew. But thanks to its Munich, Pilsner, and Vienna malt bill, it also has a caramel, biscuity sweetness that keeps the prodigious hopping in check.

APA: AOTEAROA PALE ALE

Tuatara Brewery, Paraparaumu, New Zealand
Type New Zealand Pale Ale Strength 5.8%

Aotearoa is the Maori word for New Zealand, and so this 'APA' is actually all about NZ hops. Wai-iti, NZ Cascade, Nelson Sauvin and Pacific Jade inject this beer with all of their various juicy, waxy, pithy or zesty qualities, and the result is something that looks and tastes more than a little like breakfast juice.

PULP

Verdant Brewing Co., Falmouth, UK
Type Double IPA Strength 8%

Take in Pulp's bright orange hue, get a whiff of its bodacious aroma, and understand that this is a beer for which subtlety is not on the cards. Inspired by hazy New England IPAs, Pulp is redolent of, yes, pulped mango flesh, as well as grapefruit juice, papaya, tangerine, and lime. Credit for the complex bouquet goes to its bill of Citra, Galaxy, Ekuanot and Columbus hops.

LAZURITE

Warpigs, Copenhagen, Denmark
Type American IPA Strength 6.8%

If you're ever in Copenhagen then do yourself a favour and head to the Warpigs Brewpub in the meat-packing district. This collaborative project between 3 Floyds and Mikkeller is home to a tasty Texas-style BBQ kitchen and after you've lined your stomach with brisket and hot links you can wash it down with a bright, crisp and citrus forward glass Lazurite, the brewpub's house IPA.

JUICY BITS

Weldwerks Brewing Co., Greeley, Colorado, USA
Type New England IPA Strength 6.7%

Greeley, Colorado might not be the beer radar like Fort Collins or Boulder are, but Weldwerks Brewing Company is doing all it can to change that with its forward-thinking beers. Juicy Bits is a modern IPA in the New England style, using Mosaic, El Dorado and Citra hops to instil notes of peach, nectarine and apricot into a beer that's so soft and juicy it's like a little liquid cuddle.

STICKY BUD

Wylam, Newcastle upon Tyne, UK
Type Double IPA Strength 8.7%

As well as the pelletised versions of Citra, Mosaic and Simcoe hops, Sticky Bud also uses 'lupulin powder', which is like a purified concentration of the useful aromatics found in hop flowers. Sticky Bud's name refers to the dank and resinous aroma this powder creates. In terms of taste, however, it's a highly drinkable, tropical cocktail of mango, lychee and coconut.

CITRA PALE ALE

YellowBelly, Wexford, Ireland
Type American Pale Ale Strength 4.8%

Ensuring that Ireland doesn't get left behind in the global hops race YellowBelly has produced its Citra Pale Ale. Mountains of North American Citra hops produce familiar notes of grapefruit zest and pine resin. The malts are dialled back in flavour to let those hop notes shine, although it does provide plenty of pillowy mouthfeel to carry those citrus flavours through to this beer's dry finish.

MOSS

Finback Brewery, Queens, New York, USA
Type Double IPA Strength 8.5%

Though this Double IPA clocks in at 8.5%, it wears its alcohol as elegantly as an evening gown. Beautifully soft, with a silky-smooth mouthfeel, it's the kind of beer you could down in five long quaffs without realising it. Floral and fresh as newly cut grass up front, it transitions into a cantaloupe sweetness, complemented by juicy orange citrus. Just enough grapefruit bitterness sees it through to a graceful conclusion.

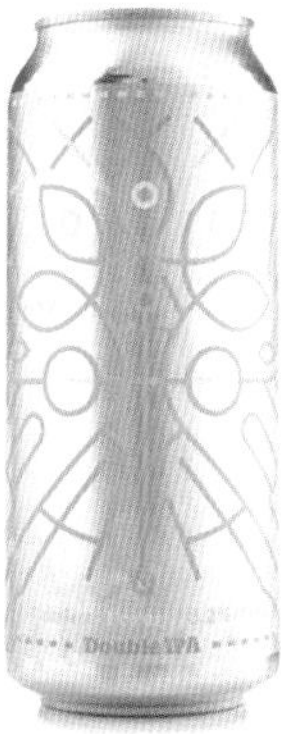

STAINLESS FOREST

Burlington Beer Company, Vermont, USA
Type Double IPA Strength 8.2%

The Platonic ideal of the New England-style Double IPA may just be this recent release by Burlington Beer Company. Stainless Forest – named after the thicket of soaring fermentation tanks found in the brewery – is hopped with Simcoe and Amarillo, and fermented with London Ale III yeast (a strain known for imparting a characteristically hazy appearance). Juicy with citrus and tropical fruits, it's also pleasingly dank and heavy on the allium notes.

FORT POINT

Bright with citrus juice and piquant with pith, this nuanced flagship pale ale makes for easy sipping

THE FACTS
Brewer Trillium Brewing Company
Origin Boston, Massachusetts, USA
Strength 6.6%
Type American Pale Ale
Web www.trilliumbrewing.com
Temperature 6-8°C

For nine long years before Trillium formally launched, co-founder JC Tetreault worked doggedly to perfect his homebrew recipes, alongside his wife Esther. When the brewery finally went pro in 2013, it didn't take long for the hype to build.

Within a few years, Trillium had expanded from a petite premises in the Fort Point neighbourhood of Boston to a second site in Canton, Massachusetts. Now, they have plans to move their original location to a 15,000 square-foot, 20-barrel brewhouse. Then there are the long-term goals of opening a farmhouse-style brewing facility in Connecticut, as well as continuing to grow its burgeoning sour and barrel-ageing programme.

What's behind the feverish rate of expansion? In a word: IPA. Alongside the likes of Tree House and Tired Hands, Trillium opened at the right time, and with the right kinds of beers, to earn itself a place square in the East Coast hype machine. Its world-class brews are murky, hop-led, dripping with juicy flavours but still beautifully nuanced.

Enter Fort Point, Trillium's signature pale ale (though, at 6.6% ABV, it could technically be described as an IPA). Brewed with Citra and Columbus hops, Fort Point delivers a punchy hit of tropical fruit on the nose and on the palate. A long sip reveals further complexities: how a touch of dankness is integrated with its citric intensity, how a small addition of resin character helps balance the brew. White wheat in the mash ensures a mouthfeel with real richness, and its appearance is all milky haze.

FRAOCH

Traditional Scottish heather ale that's the perfect accompaniment to haggis

THE FACTS
Brewer Williams Brothers Brewing Co
Origin Alloa, Scotland, UK
Strength 5%
Type Heather Ale
Web www.williamsbrosbrew.com
Temperature 8-10°C

It's quite bold of Alloa's Willam Brothers to refer to its Fraoch Heather ale as "the original craft beer" but when you consider that it's based on a recipe that is 4,000 years old it becomes difficult to argue. As they put it, they are the guardians of this ancient Gaelic recipe known as 'Leann Fraoch' which means 'Heather Ale' and as such claim to be the only brewery in the world still producing this historic recipe.

Williams Brothers claim that Heather Ales emerged in Scotland as historically Scottish brewers could not get hold of hops, which were and still are mostly grown in the southeastern English county of Kent. Instead, they turned to a variety of other ingredients to preserve and flavour their beer and heather was one of the most popular. Williams Brothers modern iteration does use First Gold hops in this beer but historically it might have featured no hops at all.

Fraoch pours a shade of light amber with, unsurprisingly, a nose of heather, which is accompanied by other floral notes of honeysuckle and lavender. There's also just a hint of peat in there too, which helps balance out this beer's floral notes. It's deliciously light to taste, which not only makes it incredibly suppable but also makes it the perfect accompaniment to the traditional Scottish dish of haggis, with the slightly spicy finish elegantly cutting through the fatty mélange of steamed offal.

GUNNAMATTA

A fragrant Earl Grey IPA that's boldly flora and beautifully citrusy

When Stu McKinlay founded Yeastie Boys with business partner Sam Possenniskie in 2008, he was also doing double-duty as a homebrew supplier. For a time, McKinlay continued to manage Liberty Brewing, until Yeastie Boys began to grow.

And grow they did – at quite the steady clip. In lieu of building their own brewing facilities, Yeastie Boys have relied on contract brewing since their founding. For a time, their brews were made exclusively at Invercargill Brewery in New Zealand, but a deal with BrewDog meant an exponential increase in output, as well as direct access to the thirsty UK market.

Of Yeastie Boys' core beers, it's Gunnamatta that's really captured the popular imagination since. An IPA that's 'dry-leafed' with Earl Grey blue flower tea, it was supposedly inspired by the pale ales and IPAs that made the overseas journey from England to the East Indies. After transporting barrels of hop-driven beers across the seas, those same ships would return from the colonies loaded with crates of spices and freshly plucked tea leaves.

When you next crack open a can of Gunnamatta, disregard the fact that the brewery describes it as smelling "like your granny's bedroom." Instead, it remains a fantastically drinkable beer – even for those who might associate floral flavours and aromas with soap or stale perfume.

In the glass, Gunnamatta pours a beautiful shade of bronze, with a lasting white head. Its aromatics proffer the expected notes of tea, as well as a touch of citrus and an appealing note of honey. On the palate, the floral character continues with a dash of jasmine, mingled with bergamot and lemon. Gunnamatta's hop flavours remain subtle throughout, though the beer offers a moreish bitterness that's almost surprising as a follow-up to its up-front bouquet. Grannies aside, Gunnamatta remains a one-of-a-kind beer that deserves to be savoured.

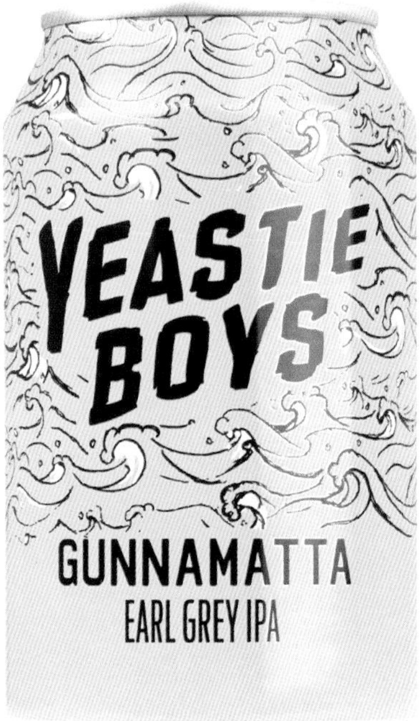

the facts

Brewer Yeastie Boys
Origin Wellington, New Zealand
Strength 6.5%
Type American IPA
Web www.yeastieboys.co.nz/
Temperature 6-8°C

"GUNNAMATTA POURS A BEAUTIFUL SHADE OF BRONZE, WITH A LASTING WHITE HEAD"

summer

Few thoughts can match the knowledge that summer is here. Little can compare to the arrival of long days, balmy evenings and the chance of some blissful sunshine. It's the time of year when your fridge really earns its keep, safeguarding those cold lagers, wheat beers and fruit beers for when you need them most.

THE WILD BEER CO
NINKASI
Saison + Bubbles + Apples + Wild Yeast
DRINK WILDLY DIFFERENT
HANDCRAFTED
STONE & WOOD
PACIFIC ALE
330mL
NO PRESERVATIVES • NO ADDITIVES
WHEAT BEER BREWED WITH SPICES
CLEAN, CRISP AND REFRESHING
BELGIAN STYLE • BOTTLE CONDITIONED
WHITE BEER
ALLAGASH
WHITE
BEER BREWED WITH SPICES
PORTLAND • MAINE
NET 12 FL. OZ.

PILSNER URQUELL

The grandfather of the modern lager style that still leaves its imitators looking like drain cleaner

Today, almost every modern, mass-produced lager can trace its roots back here, to the town of Plzen in the Czech Republic. The definitive pilsner style of lager, with its crisp, flavoursome taste and sparkling light appearance, is the benchmark against which other lagers have since aspired and carefully imitated. This humble, Bohemian town never meant to change the world of beer, though; all they wanted was something decent to drink.

It came about in a perfect storm. In the late 1830s the beer in Plzen was so awful it caused a band of leading townsfolk to revolt and form their own brewery. They invited Joseph Groll to become the brewmaster and they tasked him with making something they could happily drink. Groll had not long returned from Britain, where pale ales were forging their own path to dominance due to the development of coke. Compared to wood or coal, coke allowed barley to be kilned without becoming tainted by smoke, which was a characteristic of the dark porter beer of the era.

Given a new brewery, pale malt and an abundance of Czech Saaz hops, it took just one more ingredient to make perfect, golden beer – the water. It's easy to overlook the importance of water in beer, but it's worth noting that it makes up most of the finished product, so it naturally has a massive impact on the flavour. The water in the Plzen region is still regarded as being amongst the softest in the world, with very low mineral levels and alkalinity. When Groll applied it to his cutting edge pale malt they came together to produce a beer that was light in colour and smooth in body.

But it didn't end there. The fermented product was then cold conditioned in wooden casks, stored deep within the subterranean cellars beneath the town of Plzen for several weeks. This lengthy maturation process was called lagering and gave us the name we apply to all similar beers today.

Pilsner Urquell still claim to use the original recipe perfected by Groll in the 1840s and mature the beer for 40 days. However, a significant concession made in the wake of modern technology is that Pilsner Urquell is no longer conditioned in oak casks on a wider scale. Nevertheless, while you're unlikely to come across it in the supermarket, they still make an unfiltered and unpasteurised version often served from wooden casks. It's maltier, sweeter and chewier than the standard version, but it's an experience that's well worth seeking out if the opportunity ever comes up.

Pilsner Urquell pours a dark gold, crystal clear beer with a dazzling white head of creamy foam and mild carbonation. The aroma is crisp and peppery, with warm, toasted malt bread and a slightly herbal kick. The supremely light and smooth body is the first thing you notice – it somehow walks a tightrope between crisp and full bodied. The flavour meanwhile is a quickly moving kaleidoscope of different flavours, swiftly emerging and disappearing, from an earthy tang and grassy barley, to honeyed malt and a bite of pepper, all leading to a bittersweet finish.

the facts

Brewer Plzensky Prazdroj
Origin Plzen, Czech Republic
Strength 4.4%
Type Pilsner Lager
Web www.pilsnerurquell.com
Temperature 4-8°C

"THE SUPREMELY LIGHT AND SMOOTH BODY IS THE FIRST THING YOU NOTICE ON THE PALATE"

SAISON LUNAIRE

Forest & Main Brewing Co.,
Bend, Oregon, USA
Type Flanders Red Ale Strength 6%

Since opening five years ago, Forest & Main has proven itself to be one versatile brewery, as adept with hazy IPAs as it is classic English bitters. But it's especially beloved for its saisons. Saison Lunaire, which pours a cheery orange hue, was aged for a spell in wine barrels; consequently it offers an unmistakably vinous character, as well as peach, citrus, and funky yeast notes.

CHAMP DU BLANC

New Glarus Brewing, New Glarus, Wisconsin, USA
Type Wild Ale Strength 10%

Some beers are so vinous they seem to straddle the divide between beer and wine. New Glarus's Champ du Blanc is one such brew. A blend of sour blonde ale and Chardonnay grapes, it's aged in barrels in the brewery's 'wild fruit cave'. The result would please any sommelier: rich with butter and vanilla notes imparted by the oak, it's balanced with a yeasty funk and elements of grape must.

BELGIAN ROSE

SweetWater Brewing Company, Atlanta, Georgia, USA
Type Wild Ale Strength 7%

SweetWater's phenomenal Belgian Rose has been in the works for three years. A Belgian-style wild ale that has been blended with Georgia-grown blackberries (at the proportion of one pound per gallon), fermented with two strains of Brettanomyces (as well as souring bacteria), and which has spent time in Cabernet and Merlot barrels, it's bright with acidity, aromatic with fruit notes, and rose-coloured in the glass.

CAMDEN HELLS LAGER

A wonderful and endlessly refreshing London-born pale lager that's so flavoursome it's almost impossible to dislike

Housed beneath the railway arches of Kentish Town West overground station is Camden Town Brewery, a celebrated leading light of the London craft beer scene. Camden Hells, the brewery's award-winning flagship lager, sums up everything great about them as a brewer: beer that is bright in clarity and flavour, with good ideas and stylish packaging.

Camden Hells' name is a nod to both Helles and Pils, and it comfortably straddles both of these categories, making for a crowd-pleasing, easy-going lager that delivers every time, whether the drinker is after refreshment or flavour. Its pale gold appearance may not blow anyone away – it looks like a lager though, which is more than enough. Its head is tight and lasting, offering an appetising lemony and bready aroma, not unlike a slice of lemon cake.

The greatest thing about Camden Hells is the way it combines the light, drinkable body of a helles lager, with the crisp, firm bitterness of a pilsner. The initial sips are simple, sweet bites of clean pilsner malt with bold, bittering hops in the finish, but with each taste, there's a little bit more flavour to it and yet, at the same time, it seems simpler and simpler.

Lagers that taste clean are ten a penny, but truly impressive lagers display a sharp clarity of flavours, sweet then bitter, which truly refresh the palate. Camden Hells is such a lager, and its increasing availability on draught as well as in bottles is a welcome sight in UK pubs. Camden Town also released an unfiltered, US-hopped version called USA Hells, which even outshone its award-winning brother.

For a food companion, Hells is perfectly partnered with an enormous, topping-laden hot dog. It will comfortably cleanse the palate of any salt and oil, whilst refreshing you enough for each delicious meaty bite to taste as good as the first.

the facts

Brewer Camden Town Brewery
Origin London, Britain
Strength 4.6%
Type Lager
Web www.camdentownbrewery.com
Temperature 4-8°C

THE BEER TALKING

JASPER CUPPAIDGE
CAMDEN TOWN BREWERY

What's the inspiration behind Camden Hells Lager?
To make an excellent lager like those that inspired us in Germany – we aim for something between a Pilsner and a Munich Helles.

What's your favourite beer to drink after work?
Hells, of course! I drink all types of beer, but always seem to wind up back at Hells.

Which beer do you wish you had made?
Maybe Sierra Nevada Pale Ale.

Which beers best demonstrate who you are as a brewery?
I think beers like USA Hells and our limited release Indian Summer Lager. Although we make all types of beer, we love opening people's eyes to new forms of lager. We take something traditional and put a new spin on it.

AUGUSTINER-BRAU LAGERBIER HELL

The classic Helles lager from an old Munich brewery

THE FACTS
Brewer Augustiner-Brau, Munich
Origin Munich, Germany
Strength 5.2%
Type Helles Lager
Web www.augustiner-braeu.de
Temperature 4-8°C

Augustiner Brau was established back in 1328, making it Munich's oldest independent brewery. It's famous for its traditional methods in the brewing of all its beers, not least its most well-known and popular brew: the Helles lager. Helles, or Hell, means 'light' in German, and these beers epitomise Bavarian lager. Augustiner is famous for putting this lager through a second maturation of several months, which many believe sets it apart from competitors. Indeed, Augustiner is so confident of the quality of its beer that it doesn't really advertise it at all.

The liquid itself is a duller hue of gold than most lagers, sharing that ever so slightly deeper shade shared by authentic pilsner. The head is full, lively and aromatic. On the nose, there's freshly baked bread, just a touch of Hallertau hop pepper and a sharp lemon zing. It's a classic combination that makes the mouth water.

From the tip of the tongue to the back of your throat, this is a proper lager, through and through. That extra maturation has made a very refined but enjoyable and satisfying beast. Soft, biscuity sweetness gives way to a full mule-kick of hop bitterness. A gentle, citrusy aftertaste tingles on the tongue. There isn't much more to it, but then, there doesn't need to be. It may be straightforward, but Augustiner Helles is just so damn classy and likeable that you don't care. This is an absolutely glorious just-got-home-beer, and gives you plenty to enjoy without any of it getting in the way of you drinking it. All it needs alongside it is some slices of ham, bread and cheese – simple, flavoursome and unpretentious, just like the beer.

OUDE GEUZE

The moreish style of Altbier comes to the fore

THE FACTS
Brewer Brouwerij 3 Fonteinen
Origin Beersel, Belgium
Strength 6%
Type Geuze
Web www.3fonteinen.be
Temperature 8-10°c

Armand Debelder and his brother Guido took over 3 Fonteinen from their father in 1982, and, despite the difficulties faced by many lambic beer producers as the style became increasingly marginalised, 3 Fonteinen built a reputation as one of the best brewers and blenders of geuze (also 'gueuze', depending where you are in Belgium) in the world, using lambics from Girardin, Boon and Lindemans as well as their own.

Of all the problems that could potentially hinder a small business, a faulty thermostat nearly spelled the end of 3 Fonteinen. 13,000 bottles of its beers exploded when the thermostat wrongly set the temperature in the warehouse to over 60°C, and many thousands more were ruined. Only through sheer determination and the support of his fellow lambic makers was Debelder able to keep his business going, and eventually get his brewery back on its feet.

By 2013, 3 Fonteinen was brewing its own lambic again, having survived a crisis that almost saw it disappear forever. In 2016, it opened a new warehouse, visitor centre and tasting room, and the business continues to go from strength to strength. There's a force to the flavours of 3 Fonteinen's lambic which mirrors the zeal, fervency, and determination that helped the brewery survive.

Its young lambic, before it is blended, is furiously sharp, with vivid funk and barnyard aromas and a palate full of grapefruit, musty oak and tart sweetness. Its rambunctiousness is tempered by time and interaction with its elders, much like some people are.

The blend of one, two and three-year-old lambics, refermented into Oude Geuze, possesses all the vibrancy of the fruity, funky young lambic, and the dry, refined character of the aged beer. And that's just when it's at its freshest. Like the brewery itself, these beers have great futures ahead of them.

ALLAGASH WHITE

A modern classic that's subtle, balanced, and wholly underrated

Amidst a sea of hugely hopped IPAs, puckering wild ales, and barrel-aged stouts, Allagash White feels almost anachronistic. Hopped with Nugget, Crystal, and Czech Saaz, it has no tropical fruits on the nose, no abiding bitterness. It's fermented only with the brewery's house yeast strain, not with Brettanomyces and Lactobacillus. And for American drinkers, it certainly isn't novel: Allagash White's recipe hasn't altered since it was first brewed back in 1995. At 22 years old, this beer is old enough to order a pint in any bar in America.

All of the above may sound denigrating. Instead, it's meant as a celebration of the qualities that make Allagash White such a comforting, deserving, and often underrated neo-classic. That it has been brewed with such consistency for decades is a remarkable feat. That it is subtly spiced with coriander and curacao orange peels – emphasis on subtly – betrays an admirable kind of restraint. That it is soft in the mouth but finishes with a refreshing dryness, that it looks a little bit like early morning sunshine in the glass, that its aroma conjures a summer breeze in a herb garden: these are the traits that make it so tremendously likeable, zeitgeist be damned.

Allagash White is versatile, and a favourite among drinkers who are new to craft beer – those who are just graduating from Blue Moon with slices of oranges plopped in the glass, say. It also pleases seasoned beer geeks who have put their palates through every rigorous challenge, only to find, after countless double IPAs, that they sometimes crave things that are straightforward and understated.

Whatever your boozy experiences and preferences: if it's been a long time since you last enjoyed a bottle of Allagash White, now is your cue to rediscover this most deserving of beers.

the facts

Brewer Allagash Brewing Company
Origin Portland, Maine, USA
Strength 5.1%
Type Witbier
Web www.allagash.com/
Temperature 5-10°C

OUDE GEUZE BLACK LABEL

The selected, supreme version of an already incredible Oude Geuze

The village of Lembeek sits beside the river Senne, where years ago over 43 breweries used to make traditional, wild-fermented ales. The village's name is thought to be the origin of the term lambic, and is the home of Brouwerij Boon, which bears the name of the man who helped revive both the brewery and the styles of lambic beers it makes.

Frank Boon could be considered master blender more than brewer. The key to any good geuze, or refermented lambic-based beer (such as kriek or framboise) is the taste of the blender, finding the equilibrium between the younger, sweeter lambics and the aged, drier lambics with the greatest depth of flavour.

First created in 2015 to celebrate the 40th anniversary of the brewery, Boon's Oude Geuze Black Label uses lambics oak-aged one, two and three years in proportions that favour the older versions, making for a drier, more intense Geuze than its regular Oude Geuze or Mariage Parfait. The third and most recent edition of Black Label, whilst slightly more full-bodied, maintains a distinctively dry palate that Black Label is known for.

Its bright golden colour is best appreciated in a proper, chunky geuze tumbler. After all, we might think of these esoteric styles as highbrow, but these were once the end-of-day beers of common labourers. Despite the bracing funk and sharpness, the dryness reminds you it is all about refreshment.

Green apple, both the flesh and the skin, are prominent, alongside oaky vanilla notes. There's acidic flourishes of grapefruit, lime and lemon in this crispy sour ale, but not like the softer flavours found in hoppy pale beers. Here those citrus fruit taste as sharp and fresh as if you had bitten into them, pith and all. It's a yearly release that's truly worth waiting for, and even better with age.

the facts

Brewer Brouwerij Boon
Origin Lembeek, Belgium
Strength 7%
Type Geuze
Web www.boon.be
Temperature 8-10°C

BROOKLYN LAGER

A true American craft beer icon that remains a pure delight

Garrett Oliver, Brooklyn's brewmaster, studied his beer craft in the UK. His education is very much on display in Brooklyn's range of beers, but their timeless Vienna-style lager is their flagship brand, and with good reason.

Vienna lagers are typically slightly darker than most other lagers, with more malty sweetness. Brooklyn's pours the colour of proper pale ale, a beautiful bronze, with a lively head that's bursting with aromas. Suddenly, your nose is in American IPA territory. Grapefruit, pine, orange peel and peach all compete for your attention, softened by a scent of warm maple syrup. Brooklyn Lager's flavour is, quite frankly: 'what you smell is what you taste.' It's all here, one after another, never getting tired or thin on the palate. Everything is where it should be: sweetness building gradually and confidently, ending cleanly and sharply with a long, exquisitely floral finish. The sharp carbonation brings every possible flavour to the fore in perfect clarity, and there is much to be enjoyed on every sip. The sense of professionalism and quality is unquestionable.

Despite all this flavour, it never becomes heavy, and if anything it lacks the bigger body of say, an IPA, to really execute all those wonderful flavours perfectly. But who cares? This is a lager, for goodness' sake. This is the spectrum of flavours that any brewer would be happy to achieve in their pale ale or their IPA.

Brooklyn Lager is the statesman of the large-scale US craft scene; a clever, genuine charmer that's travelled broadly and can still teach a thing or two to the modern upstarts in brewing. There are few easier food matches in the world of beer than putting a bottle of Brooklyn Lager alongside a freshly-baked Italian pizza. Don't worry about the toppings though, just relax and let the beer do the work for you.

the facts

Brewer Brooklyn Brewery
Origin New York City, USA
Strength 5.3%
Type Lager
Web www.brooklynbrewery.com
Temperature 4-8°C

PETRUS AGED PALE

Tart & funky wood-aged pale ale that was a favourite of Michael Jackson

THE FACTS
Brewer Brouwerij De Brabandere
Origin Kortrijk, Belgium
Strength 7.3%
Type Foederbier
Web www.brouwerijdebrabandere.be
Temperature 10-12 °C

These days De Brabandere's Petrus Aged Pale is one of the most popular beers in its range. However, there was a time when the brewery didn't sell it to the public at all. Thinking it would be too sour and tart for local palates it instead served it blended with its sweeter Aged Red and Bruin. It would take a fated visit from the famous beer writer Michael Jackson to change this forever.

On a visit to the brewery, in Kortrijk, which lies in the West Flanders region of Belgium near the French border, Jackson asked to taste the unblended beer straight from one of the large oak foeders in which the beer is aged. He enjoyed the beer so much he asked where he could buy some to share with friends and was told it was not for sale. Refusing to budge, Jackson asked how much he needed to buy in order to take some home to the UK and the brewery ended up selling him an entire vat of the beer. Such was the increased popularity once Jackson brought this beer back with him that it became part of the brewery's core range.

Aged Pale spends two years maturing in oak, picking up sharp, tart flavours imbued by the culture of yeast and bacteria that resides within the wood. If you've not tried it before, its sourness can come as a little bit of a shock, but your palate will adjust after two or three sips. If it's still too sour then blending it in the glass with a Petrus Aged Red or Bruin will soften those sour notes with a hint of sweetness.

JEVER PILSENER

The definitive German take on the classic style

THE FACTS
Brewer Friesisches Brauhaus ze Jever
Origin Jever, Germany
Strength 4.9%
Type Pilsner Lager
Web www.jever.de
Temperature 4-8°C

The Jever Brewery had a tough time of it to begin with. It was founded in 1848 by Diedrich Konig, in the Friesland region of north Germany. Konig died in 1867, leaving it to his son who sold it on to Theo Fetkoter. The brewery was modernised and in 1887 a well was dug to provide the superb water which defines Jever to this day. Fetkoter's son later took over but the beginnings of the Fetkoter brewing dynasty were smashed when the new owner was killed in World War I. The Jever Brewery has since changed hands between larger brewing groups several times over the past century. It is now owned by the Radeberger Group, a subsidiary of the Oetker Group.

Jever Pilsener (pronounced yay-ver) is well carbonated, with a colour like liquid gold – any paler and it would be invisible, apart from the modest, dimpled head of white foam. It produces a pleasant aroma of grassy barley, freshly baked bread and peppercorns.

The taste is striking for being both bitter and incredibly soft. The Hallertau and Tettnang hops bring on an earthy, tangy bitterness which is restrained by the pale malt's contribution of Melba toast, dry crackers and whispers of fluffy, fresh baked white bread. Hallertau and Tettnang are soon back to ply your palate with peppery spice, earthiness and hedgerow woodiness. The finish is the best part, a grassy, drying astringency which lingers and teases you to drink more.

It's the perfect end to the working day and the start of a chilled out evening.

OUDE KRIEK

Brouwerij 3 Fonteinen, Beersel, Belgium

Type Kriek Strength 6%

• Released in yearly vintages from this highly respected brewer and blender of Lambic beers, 3 Fonteinen's Oude Kriek is made using local cherries steeped in young lambic for up to eight months, and undergoes spontaneous fermentation. Its flavour is rich yet light, with deep, natural cherry and almond notes, juicy sweetness and refreshing, fruity acidity. A tart and tasty masterpiece.

PALETAS PRICKLY PEAR

5 Rabbit Cerveceria, Chicago, Illinois, USA

Type Fruit Wheat Beer Strength 5.3%

• With this summer seasonal, 5 Rabbit Cerveceria turns paletas – Mexican ice lollies, made with fresh juice and pieces of fruit – into liquid refreshment. But despite that association (and what the beer's jubilant shade of pink might suggest), Paletas isn't a sugar bomb. Instead, this prickly pear-laced wheat beer is tart, ever so slightly saline, and ideal for scorching summer days.

ATRIAL RUBICITE

Jester King Brewery, Austin, Texas, USA

Type Wild Ale Strength 5.2%

• Now in its seventh edition, Atrial Rubicite remains one of Jester King's most popular beers. A phenomenal quantity of raspberries (5.2 pounds per gallon) go into this ruby-red sour beer, which is fermented with farmhouse yeast, souring bacteria, and yeast strains hailing from Texas Hill Country. The result is ripe, jammy, and beautifully tart.

TIPOPILS

Birrificio Italiano, Italy

Type Pilsner Strength 5.2%

• This robust Italian example of pilsner pulls off the difficult trick of extracting juicy citrus flavours from humble European hops. Its appetising haze and delightful, fruity aroma are matched by a rich, crisp body. The malt provides a sweet and simple stage for the beer's pronounced hop character that begins sharp and floral, before evolving into something fruitier, pithier, and more bitter.

HACKER-PSCHORR OKTOBERFEST MARZEN

Hacker-Pschorr, Munich, Germany

Type Lager Strength 5.8%

• Marzens are lagers brewed in March and matured until Oktoberfest. Hacker-Pschorr's is beautifully coppery, with a thick, tight head offering a sickly sweet aroma. There is just enough toffee sweetness, and an almost nutty dryness to it that is normally found in English best bitter. The complexity never gets in the way of the liquid's drinkability, and its strength is reined in nicely by a delicate but balanced palate of sharp, bitter and sweet.

DOGPATCH SOUR

Almanac Beer Co., San Francisco, California, USA

Type American Sour Ale Strength 7.5%

• Almanac's Farm to Barrel series comes in a vast range of guises, from heavily hopped to graciously fruited. At its core sits Dogpatch Sour, named for the part of San Francisco the brewery calls home. This deeply red sour beer pulls acidic notes from cherries that are eased out by barrel ageing in red wine barrels, adding vinous character and dry, tannic finish to this accomplished beer.

WILD WEST

Brouwerij Alvinne, Moen, Belgium

Type Wild Ale Strength 6%

• A collaboration between Alvinne and American brewer Stillwater Artisanal, this barrel-aged sour beer demonstrates elegant interplay between yeast and oak notes. Eight months in Bordeaux red wine barrels adds decadent grape must and tannic oak character, lightened by tartness, fruit and acidity. A complex beer with real potential for ageing to allow its sharper flavours to mellow.

FOEDER GOLD

American Solera, Tulsa, Oklahoma, USA

Type Wild Ale Strength 5.6%

• Aged in an American oak foeder with Brettanomyces and several souring cultures, American Solera's Foeder Gold is a surprisingly refreshing and quaffable wild ale. Rather than a sharp hit of acidity, its sourness is light and beautifully integrated. Have a sip, and you will also pick up on light grain, a bit of lemon brightness, and the gentlest hint of barnyardy funk.

BRINEY MELON GOSE

Anderson Valley Brewing Company,
Boonville, California, USA
Type Gose Strength 4.2%

• Anderson Valley's Briney Melon Gose is about as close as beer gets to resembling a cocktail. Redolent of summery watermelon and seriously saline, it could almost be served in a salt-rimmed glass with a shot of tequila on the side. But on its own, this quenching and lightly sour beer, with its bright acidity and dry finish, remains an excellent candidate for dog-day afternoons spent in the sun.

PJ FRUH KOLSCH

Brauerei Früh Am Dom, Cologne, Germany
Type Kolsch Strength 4.8%

• Fruh's version of Cologne's famous beer takes the delicacy and crispness of the style to new heights. It shines brightly in the glass, and generates an enormous amount of head. A soft, lemony and malty aroma of bread and a little spice gets the mouth watering. Its flavour is so clean, so soft and delightfully floral that it's hard to pin down the many subtle flavours that appear without drinking it all too quickly.

HIBISCUS TEA GOSE

Arizona Wilderness Brewing Co.,
Gilbert, Arizona, USA
Type Gose Strength 4.8%

• Hibiscus is the key ingredient in agua de jamaica – a refreshing, sweet-tart Mexican 'aqua fresca'. In this piquant beer, Arizona Wilderness borrows the flavour profile from agua de jamaica, adds Arizona-grown tangelos, coriander, and salt to the mix, plus fistfuls of Galaxy, Citra, and Amarillo hops. The result is candied, floral, lightly acidic, and delicately saline, making it the ideal beverage for summer days.

RHUBOISE

Brekeriet, Landskrona, Sweden
Type Wild Ale Strength 6%

• Brekeriet was founded by three brothers in 2015. Since then, it's already carved out an international reputation for its rustic, farmhouse-style beers, all of which make use of Brettanomyces. With Rhuboise, the brewery adds copious quantities of rhubarb and raspberries to a wild ale base during secondary fermentation, making for a hazy, peach-hued brew that offers plenty of fruit on the palate, and just a whiff of yeasty musk.

LA LUNA ROSSA

Birrificio del Ducato, Busseto (PR), Italy
Type Sour / Wild Ale Strength 8%

• La Luna Rossa from Italy's Birrificio del Ducato is comprised of a blend of Krisopolis, a two-year-old barrel aged sour, which is then blended with Morello cherries, and Ultimata Luna, an Amarona barrel matured Barley Wine also aged with cherries. If that hasn't got your juices flowing then pouring it into a glass to release the crimson beer along with intense cherry aromas almost certainly will.

GASTON

Burning Sky Brewery, Firle, East Sussex, UK
Type Belgian Pale Ale Strength 6%

• Burning Sky is well-known for producing Belgian-style beers with subtlety, finesse and technical accomplishment. Gaston, a Belgian-style pale ale, is no different, weaving together its New and Old World hop character, fruity yeast notes and a dry, crisp texture with aplomb. Its most impressive characteristic, however, is its sheer drinkability, retaining its clarity of flavour to the very last drop.

SANG NOIR

Cascade Brewing,Portland, Oregon, USA
Type American Wild Ale Strength 10.1%

• Sang Noir is a deep, red-hued beer that spends the beginning of its lifespan maturing in bourbon barrels that have also been filled with Bing cherries. Expect notes of port, cherry, vanilla and oak rounded out by a mouth-puckering sourness that will have you gasping for another sip.

AMARILLO SOUR

Chorlton Brewing Company, Manchester, UK
Type Sour Pale Ale Strength 5.4%

• Based on the sour pale beers of Prussia and Saxony, Chorlton's best-known beer incorporates the refreshing sharpness of Berlinner Weisse and the tropical fruit aromas of American pale ale. It's a delicate balance – one that this beer achieves, with citrus and pineapple offsetting the sour flavours, without losing any refreshing tartness.

Budweiser Budvar

Budweiser Budvar Brewery, Czech Republic
Type Lager Strength 5%

Within the brewing industry there are few fights more contentious than ownership of the famous Budweiser name. You've no doubt heard of Budweiser – the King of Beers, mass marketed by AB-InBev. But there's also an entirely separate Budweiser, produced in the Czech Republic. Both claim original ownership and both have the right to use it, though Budvar is sold as Czechvar in the United States. We're not taking sides here. Buy one of each and let yourself decide who should be crowned the King of Beers.

Bretta Rose

Firestone Walker Brewing Company, Buellton, California, USA
Type Wild Ale Strength 5.3%

Though Firestone Walker is headquartered in Paso Robles, its Barrelworks facility is located almost 100 miles south in Buellton. Aside from being a good way to prevent any Brettanomyces cross-contaminations, it also allows the brewery space to produce stunners like Bretta Rosé. A Berliner weisse that's aged in French oak puncheons for six months before a secondary wild fermentation with 1,000 pounds of local raspberries, it's perfumed, complex, and absolutely sensational.

Emerson's Pilsner

Emerson's, Dunedin, New Zealand
Type Pilsner Strength 4.9%

New Zealand hops share similar flavour characteristics with the grapes that have made it such a famous wine nation. Emerson's, based in Dunedin on the South Island, create a genre-defining example of the style. Expect kiwi fruit, gooseberry and passion fruit, followed by a crisp, dry finish.

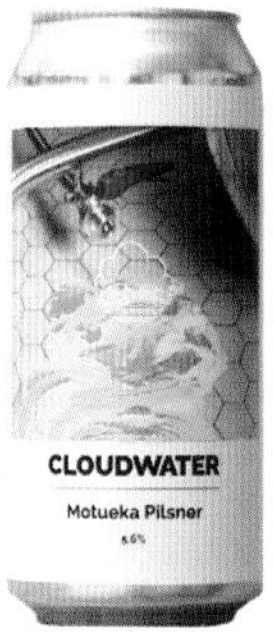

Motueka Pilsner

Cloudwater Brew Co, Manchester, UK
Type Pilsner Strength 5.6%

Whilst best known for Double IPAs, Cloudwater have also excelled in brewing less boisterous styles. Their Motueka Pilsner demonstrates a keen understanding of how a clean, dry and bitter lager should work, before deftly using New Zealand hop Motueka to add waxy citrus notes to increase its refreshment factor even further.

Schiehallion

Harviestoun, Clackmannanshire, Scotland
Type Lager Strength 4.8%

Schiehallion (pronounced she-hal-e-on) is a cask conditioned lager that's also available in bottles. It's managed to win awards at CAMRA festivals, which is no easy feat as they're a crowd who often view lager with suspicion (it is the Campaign for Real Ale, after all). It's a hop forward, floral lager, with citrus, cut grass and honey notes. It all adds up to a lager that gets on famously with ale and lager lovers alike.

Rhythm Rug

Fonta Flora Brewery, Morganton, North Carolina, USA
Type Wild Ale Strength 5.9%

Fonta Flora is famous for using local ingredients to create beers with a true sense of place. Recently, it has even purchased a farm on which to grow ingredients, and the next phase of the brewery. Rhythm Rug is a wild ale brewed with large amounts of local strawberries. Its funky nose and rich, natural strawberry flavour is accented with refreshing acidity.

Gueuze (Black Label)

Brouwerij Girardin, Sint Ulriks-Kapelle, Belgium
Type Gueuze Strength 5%

Girardin traces its family ownership back to 1882, and provides lambic to other blenders of gueuze, including 3 Fonteinen. Its unfiltered, unpasteurised Black Label gueuze is blended from lambics aged 12, 18 and 24 months. When fresh it has an almost peach-like fruitiness and floral aroma; older bottles have more pronounced wild yeast notes and flavours of grape and apple skin.

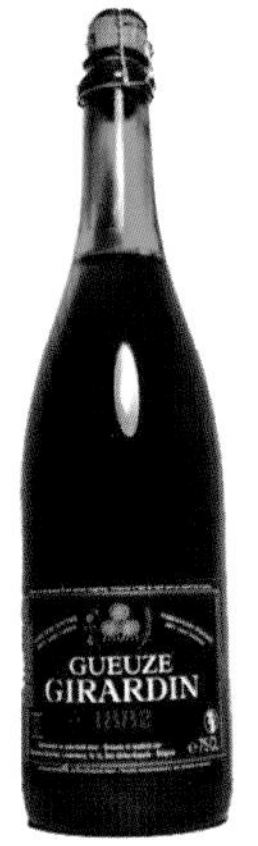

Key Lime Tau

Hawkshead Brewery, Cumbria, UK
Type Wild Ale Strength 6.28%

The 2015 Rainbow Project, pairing seven UK brewers with American counterparts to brew colour-inspired collaborations, saw Hawkshead create this green-inspired beer with Crooked Stave. This mixed fermentation, oak-aged beer also uses lime zest and lactose. A delicious blend of creaminess, sharp citric zing and moreish tartness has made it popular enough to be rebrewed several times.

VICTORY PRIMA PILS

Victory Brewing, USA

Type Pilsner Lager Strength 5.3%

• Considered to be one of the finest American craft lagers, Victory Prima Pils blends traditional Czech ingredients with the American fetish for hopping the hell out of everything. Sweet, caramel malt vies for your attention against a lush, citrus and green grass aroma. Grapefruit, herbaceous hops and bread arrive on the palate and lead to a resurgence of the grassy hop in the dry, not-too-bitter finish.

EVERETT

Hill Farmstead, Greensboro, Vermont, USA

Type Porter Strength 7.5%

• Forming part of Hill Farmstead brewery's ancestral series, Everett is a porter brewed in honour of the brother of founder Shaun Hill's Grandfather. Everett fuses roasted malts imported from Germany and the UK with American hops to conjure forth notes of bitter dark chocolate, pipe tobacco and freshly brewed coffee that lead to a dry, mineral finish.

ZURE VAN TILDONK

Hof Ten Dormaal, Tildonk, Belgium

Type Wild Ale Strength 6%

• Founded less than a decade ago, and based out of a farmstead in rural Belgium, Hof Ten Dormaal is making its beers the traditional way. The brewery roasts its own malt, grows its own hops, and sources wild yeast from the open air. Zure Van Tildonk, a lemony sour beer that spends a year in barrels prior to release, is quenchable, dry, and a perfect expression of the area's terroir.

KIWI RISING

Jack's Abby Brewing, Massachusetts, USA

Type Double IPL Strength 8.5%

• In the New England brewing scene, Jack's Abby distinguishes itself by focusing exclusively on lagers. Its offerings range from sour wheat lagers to classic pilsners, but one of its most coveted releases is the seasonal Kiwi Rising. Made with heaping quantities of New Zealand hops, including four kettle additions and several dry hop additions, it's intensely juicy and fruit-forward but still impeccably clean.

RUNNING WITH SCEPTRES

Lost and Grounded Brewers, Bristol, UK

Type India Pale Lager Strength 5.2%

• In stark contrast to its other, noble hopped lager, Keller Pils, Bristol's Lost and Grounded also produce a stunningly vibrant and juicy American hopped lager known as Running with Sceptres. This 'special lager beer' as they call it, is beaming with the scent of fresh lemon peel, cantaloupe and mango. These flavours find balance in soft, biscuit malts and a thirst-quenchingly dry finish.

TZATZIKI SOUR

Mad Hatter Brewing Company, Liverpool, UK

Type Berliner Weisse Strength 4.5%

• At first blush, a sour beer designed to imitate the flavour profile of tzatziki sauce sounds challenging. But consider that Lactobacillus is also used to sour yogurt and cheese – and that a bit of lactic tang can be a refreshing thing in a beer. Add in cucumber and mint soaked in ouzo, and you're left with a brew that can refresh on the most sweltering days of summer.

KELLER PILS

Lost and Grounded Brewers, Bristol, UK

Type Kellerbier Strength 4.6%

• Whilst Lost and Grounded may only recently have celebrated its first anniversary, the brewing experience and skill of co-founder Alex Troncoso is communicated loud and clear in its Keller Pils. The knowledge of what makes this style so wonderful – the refined simplicity of pale grain, noble hops, and lengthy conditioning – is more than evident in this quenchingly dry, bready and delicately peppery lager.

Z12 SVETLY LEZAK

Pivovar Kout na Šumav, Kout na Šumave, Czech Republic

Type Czech Pilsner Strength 5%

• In a country where the recipe for Svetlý Ležák (pale lager) is almost written in stone, the main variable is the brewery itself. The Šumava forest that Kout calls home has a history associated with magic and legend, which might be why its light, airy, lemony and peppery 12° lager has a habit of becoming the only beer you want to drink.

FOU'FOUNE

A floral, brightly acidic, and jubilant expression of apricot

the facts

Brewer Brasserie Cantillon
Origin Brussels, Belgium
Strength 5%
Type Lambic
Web www.cantillon.be
Temperature 12-15°C

Where do you begin with a beer like Fou'Foune? Securing a bottle of this elusive apricot lambic feels like holding a rare treasure in your hands. Not that that's an unusual sensation when it comes to Cantillon, which remains one of the most celebrated breweries in the world for its traditional approach to lambics and gueuzes.

Founded in 1900 and now led by fourth-generation brewer Jean Van Roy, Cantillon sets the world gold standard for wild, spontaneously fermented beers. After each brew, its wort sits in copper coolships where it's exposed to the area's microflora, before being transferred to oak or chestnut casks and aged. The brewery's classic gueuze – a blend of lambics of different ages – makes up roughly half of its output, while the rest comprises a range of fruit lambics. Of these, Fou'Foune remains one of the brewery's most popular, and most coveted; after its Kriek and Rosé de Gambrinus, it is also the third highest-volume fruit lambic that Cantillon produces.

To make Fou'Foune, Cantillon ships in 1,200kg of highly perfumed and aromatic Bergeron apricots from France each summer, which offer a wonderful mingling of sweetness and tartness. The fruits are added to a lambic base, where they infuse for a period of five weeks – just enough for the apricots to have broken down and imparted their sun-drenched bouquet to the brew.

When fresh, Fou'Foune – which pours bronze-gold – is a marvel, rich with notes of apricot, peach, citrus zest, and undergirded by a thrumming, yeasty complexity. As the years go by, its fruit-forward sweetness recedes, while the intensity of its acidity and funk mounts. If you're lucky enough to have a few bottles, taste a younger batch next to one that's spent a few years in your cellar to best appreciate how this beer matures, how it deepens and becomes even more complex.

SCHNEIDER MEINE HOPFENWEISSE (TAP5)

From US German rivalry came one of the world's best wheat beers

Meine Hopfenweisse was originally a collaborative competition of sorts. New York's Brooklyn Brewery and Schneider decided to each brew a Hopfenweisse and see which was best. Brooklyn's used American hops of course, creating big, citrusy, resinous flavours of tropical fruit. Schneider managed to achieve something similar, better in fact, using just native German hop varieties in generous quantities. Tap 5, as it came to be known, is now a regular brew at Schneider, which is something that everyone can be thankful for.

Meine Hopfenweisse has that same luminescent, coppery glow as other Schneider wheat beers, so much so it sometimes seems to be a source of light. The banana notes are certainly there, but they are joined by apricot, lime and lemon, not just essences or aromas, but pulped, sticky and juicy. There's a slightly wild, farmyard note of hay behind it all, as if the beer is trying to physically transport you to the end of summer in a wheat field in Germany.

Taking a mouthful is like biting into a creamy, fruity cheesecake. Honey-sweetened biscuits folded into soft lemon meringue, followed by a firm, earthy bite of hops that leaves the palate not only refreshed but craving for more. The beer's formidable strength is not so much a defining characteristic, just a pleasing coincidence that never gets in the way of its flavour. It's one of the best wheat beers in the world.

It's difficult to imagine matching this beer to anything other than the lemon-and-lime cheesecake it bears such a resemblance to, but it also goes quite nicely with meringues, providing they have a thick, syrupy sauce. A meaty, flavoursome fish like monkfish or sea bass can also pair well with this incredible weissbier, but anything lighter will simply be swept aside by its sensational flavour.

the facts

Brewer Weisse Brauhaus G. Schneider & Sohn
Origin Kelheim, Germany
Strength 8.2%
Type Wheat Beer
Web www.schneider-weisse.de
Temperature 4-8°C

SINCE 1040
BAYERISCHE STAATSBRAUEREI
Brewed and bottled by
Bayerische Staatsbrauerei
Weihenstephan
Germany
THE WORLD'S OLDEST BREWERY
SINCE 1040
BAYERISCHE STAATSBRAUEREI
Weihenstephan
HEFE
WEISSBIER
alc 5.4% vol
CLOUDY WHEAT BEER

WEIHENSTEPHAN HEFE WEISSBIER

An aromatic wheat beer that's straightforward, simple and sublime

Few beers can boast a heritage as long as Weihenstephaner, which has been brewing on the same site for nearly a thousand years. Atop Nährberg Hill in the Bavarian city of Freising in roughly 720, Saint Korbinian founded a church of Saint Stephen, which became a monastery roughly a hundred years later. When brewing began there in 1040, it had become a Benedictine abbey, and beer has been brewed there ever since.

Now known as the Bavarian State Brewery Weihenstephan, their Hefe Weissbier is a seminal example of the style, and a superb baseline wheat beer experience. It pours a glorious, burnished gold colour in the glass, with the very lively carbonation and mountains of aromatic head that are typical of the style. The head is naturally thick, creamy and dense, forming interesting cloud shapes as it recedes. The nose is textbook hefeweiss – banana, bubblegum, cloves – but with a pleasing and appetising pepperiness.

The first taste is a bit of a shock, not in its flavour, but its texture. The sudden bursts of banana, caramel and bubblegum, followed up with spicy punches of clove and nutmeg, are feisty and lip-smacking. When the finish arrives, it dries out gently into lemons and spice. The high carbonation and potent smack of spicy bitterness make future tastes just as sharp and snappy.

Many commercially produced wheat beers become a little thin or too yeasty towards the end, a common problem for overly sweet pale beers, but Weihenstephan Hefeweiss manages to stay fresh and clean all the way down. This is a testament to the beer's quality and consistent freshness. It's the kind of pint that doesn't sit neglected on the table; it's in your hand after that first taste, and nothing is going to persuade you to put it down. It's an impressive all-rounder: full, sweet, fresh and crisp, with sharp elbows and plenty of bite.

the facts

Brewer Weihenstephan
Origin Bavaria, Germany
Strength 5.4%
Type Wheat beer
Web www.weihenstephaner.de
Temperature 8-12°C

INTERVIEW
MARIO SCHÄFER
WEIHENSTEPHAN

What's the inspiration/heritage behind Weihenstephan's Pilsner and Weissbier?
Both of these beer types have a long tradition in Bavaria. But some breweries, especially the bigger ones in Germany, started to change their recipes to reach a big group of buyers.

But due to this change, some beers lost parts of their character.

For Pilsner and Weissbier, we want to create beers with a unique character in dependence of these old beer styles. The Weissbier has the typical aromatic flavour of banana and clove.

The Pilsner is still made in a traditional way which was unique in Germany for a long time. It has a refined, refreshing taste and a hoppy head.

Our intention is to brew beers with a perfect drinkability. If a person orders two glasses of our beer in a bar and afterwards he wants to order one more, we know we did a good job. We like the challenge of creating good beers with water, malt, hops and yeast, to create beers with a constant quality. That's the art of brewing.

Which Weihenstephan beer best demonstrates who you are as a brewery?
Our flagship beer is our Hefeweissbier, but all our beers represent the way of life in Weihenstephan. We brew in the tradition of an old brewery with the inspiration to create interesting beers like Infinium, for example.

SCHNEIDER AVENTINUS (TAP6)

A deep, dark and unnerringly complex weissbier with an epic taste

Weissbiers are a category that some people can find to be a little samey. Every now and again, something spectacular comes along and changes your whole perception of the style; Schneider Weisse Aventinus is such a beer. Named after Johannes Aventinus, a highly regarded historian of Bavaria in the 16th century, 'Tap 6' (as it is sometimes known) is a Weizendoppelbock that is dark, powerful and frankly incredible.

As wheat beers go, this really is as dark as it gets. With a deep, ruby-mahogany of impenetrable cloudiness, it wears a fierce, tall tan head like a crown. The aroma is in your sinuses long before the glass even reaches your nose. Handfuls of freshly baked rum-soaked fruitcake, bananas, mulled wine and dark chocolate burst from the foam, tinged with a perfumey boozeyness that is intoxicating in itself.

Where most wheat beers slickly slide across the palate in a creamy waltz of gentle spices and light, estery fruit, Aventinus comes stomping in in a violent polka; a bombing campaign of dark fruit, alcohol and chocolate. A lip-smacking creaminess binds these powerful flavours as they transform into a finish of epic proportions. Toffee, banana, even whisky or port-like notes of alcohol all sound together in one long hum of warming goodness.

For all its complexity. This is a rich, endlessly delicious and rewarding beer that just keeps on giving with every sip. People who think weissbier is a samey style can get their synapses rewired by this dark, treacly, fruity monster.

the facts

Brewer Weisse Brauhaus G. Schneider & Sohn
Origin Kelheim, Germany
Strength 8.2%
Type Wheat beer
Web www.schneider-weisse.de
Temperature 4-8°C

SPONTANBASIL

A bright, herbaceous, and beautifully tart lambic infused with fresh basil leaves

What happens when a classic Belgian brewery, founded in 1822, teams up with an itinerant brewery established in Copenhagen in 2006? You end up with a truly unusual, old-meets-new brew like SpontanBasil. A traditional lambic – except for the fact that it's aged on oak alongside fistfuls of fragrant basil leaves – SpontanBasil is bright, tart, and gloriously redolent of the herb.

As the largest independent, family-run lambic brewery in the world, Lindemans knows a thing or two about spontaneous fermentation. That expertise attracted Mikkeller founder Jeppe Borg Bjergsø, whose Spontan Series of fruit-infused, spontaneous fermentation beers betrays a similar interest. Together, they devised the recipe for SpontanBasil: a blend of one-to-two year old lambics that's aged on oak alongside whole basil leaves.

Some have, rather uncharitably, likened the experience of sipping SpontanBasil to eating whole spoonfuls of pesto, but in actuality, this beer succeeds because it isn't savoury. In the glass, it pours a luminous bronze-gold, and its heady aroma is bright with basil but also piquant with lemon zest.

On the palate, SpontanBasil shows all the nuance of a classic lambic, with its tartness and its subtle funk; against this traditional base, the basil is all the more surprising. It seems a coup that the brewers have managed to capture the essence of the plant, without any vegetal flavours, any loss of volatile aromatic compounds. Instead, SpontanBasil offers the pure essence of basil, almost floral in its bright purity. Close your eyes and sip and you might as well have stumbled into some sun-drenched wild basil patch on a summer's day.

While SpontanBasil is absolutely enjoyable on its own, this supremely food-friendly beer also makes for an exceptional accompaniment to a meal. Serve it alongside a caprese salad, a Margherita pizza, or yes, a plate of pesto-drenched pasta to really appreciate its culinary potential.

the facts

Brewer Lindemans Brewery and Mikkeller
Origin Vlezenbeek, Belgium and Copenhagen, Denmark
Strength 5.5%
Type Lambic
Web www.lindemans.be/
Temperature 5-7°C

HITACHINO NEST WHITE ALE

Behind the florid motif lies a precision-brewed ale

THE FACTS
Brewer Kiuchi Brewery
Origin Naka, Japan
Strength 5.5%
Type Wit Beer
Web www.hitachinonest.com
Temperature 4-8°C

Hitachino Nest beers are starting to appear in many craft beer bars and shops, and have quickly and rightly earned a reputation. Each of their bottles stand out on the shelf. Their packaging is curiously ornate, adorned with elaborate typefacing and small owls, suggesting something whimsical or irreverent. The truth is that every one of Hitachino Nest's beers are precision-brewed, subtle and exciting to drink.

Sold in either a 330ml or mighty 720ml bottle, perfect for sharing, this White Ale pours a soft, cloudy gold, with a thick, weissbier head. The classic notes of baking bread and lemon sit comfortably alongside the advertised coriander and orange peel. Nutmeg also makes an appearance, but as a very soft afterthought.

The first sip lays a foundation of cheesecake-base and sweet-yet-sour orange peel. A further taste builds on this, adding layers of lemon zest, sweeter orange and spicy, tingling nutmeg that stick around and develop into an almost ginger-like finish. The body seems too thin at first, but this allows the subtlety of the flavours to shine.

This is a beer that's destined for food matching, make no mistake. Weiss and witbier can be adaptable in this regard, but the best thing to match Hitachino Nest White Ale with is something as subtle as itself. Salmon, preferably sashimi, and light, creamy desserts become poetry when paired with this spectacularly understated beer. Hitachino Nest beers will almost certainly cost more, but be in no doubt that they are a seriously rewarding investment.

ON SKINS: PLUMS

A unique 'Urban Farmhouse' fruit beer

THE FACTS
Brewer Redchurch Brewery
Origin London, UK
Strength 6.5%
Type Fruit Sour
Web www.redchurch.beer
Temperature 6-8°C

Redchurch's James Rylance has had as prolific and varied a career as a London brewer could hope for. Starting out at The Kernel, he has since been Head Brewer at Beavertown and now at Redchurch, with a brief stint making wine thrown in for good measure.

Rylance joined Redchurch during a massive expansion, which has seen the brewery successfully crowdfund towards, build and open a new production facility just outside of London. The brewery's original site in Bethnal Green has now been given over entirely to Rylance to produce spontaneously fermented, barrel-aged, or fruited beers in a project Redchurch calls 'Urban Farmhouse'.

On Skins: Plums, as its name suggests, forms part of an ongoing series of beers aged on fruit, in this case plums picked from the National Orchard Collection in Brogdale, Kent. The plums are all foot-pressed, as a winemaker would do with grapes, and added skin, flesh, stone and all into barrels of beer soured with lactic acid bacteria and aged for four months. The beer itself has the vibrant colour of the plum flesh, deeply hazy and almost luminescent.

The depth of flavour is phenomenal – lush plum notes and invigoratingly sour edges wrapped around a light, zesty and spritzy texture that recalls a Mimosa cocktail more than a beer. Tannic, wine-like notes last long into the finish, and there seems to be more to explore and discover with each sip.

MAHRS BRAU PILSNER

Mahrs Bräu, Bamberg, Germany

Type Pilsner Strength 4.9%

• The cosy Bamberg brewpub that Mars Bräu calls home is a must visit location for any budding beer tourist – proving instantly than there is more to this German town than just rauchbier. Mahrs Pilsner pours a brilliant shade of yellow and is capped with a satisfyingly tight head of foam. Noble Hallertauer hops add a herbal, grassy snap to bready malts to create a pilsner that is simply exceptional.

FOXBIC

Mill's Brewing, Somerset, UK

Type Sour/Farmhouse Ale Strength 4.7%

• Foxbic is a deviously clever beer that is a blend of both a beer that is not dissimilar to a Belgian lambic and Foxwhelp apple juice from cider guru Tom Oliver. The beer then spends eight months fermenting in oak with cider lees and the result is quite spectacular. Golden Delicious apple flavours shine through, which are underpinned by a mouth-puckering, lactic sourness that's as dry as a bone at the finish

NEAPOLITAN PALE ALE

Northern Monk Brew Co, Leeds, UK

Type Milkshake Pale Ale Strength 5.9%

• Fitting considering today's trend for hazy, lactic-rich, fruit-forward beers, Northern Monk's Neapolitan Pale Ale is as nostalgic as a childhood stop at the ice cream van. Modelled on the classic Neapolitan trifecta, the beer is brewed with additions of lactose, strawberries, and chocolate sauce. But rather than muddied or over-sweet, this beer boasts a lusciously creamy mouthfeel, gentle hopping, and a whisper of desserty decadence.

ICE CREAM IPA CLOUDBERRY

Omnipollo and Buxton Brewery, Sweden/UK

Type Milkshake IPA Strength 7.2%

• A standout in the ongoing, collaborative Ice Cream IPA series between Omnipollo and Buxton, this version made little-known cloudberries its fruity muse. Like large, golden raspberries in appearance, cloudberries hail from Scandinavia and have a beguiling, vinous sweetness. When brewed with lactose and vanilla, as they are here, the result is rich, jammy, and floral.

PILLAR OF SALT

Redchurch Brewery, London, UK

Type Gose Strength 4.5%

• In addition to a core range of 'clean' hoppy and dark beers under its main branding, London brewer Redchurch has an Urban Farmhouse project for its numerous mixed fermentation projects, including this excellent and accomplished German-style sour wheat beer, brewed with salt and coriander. The herbal notes are delicate, but there is serious salinity to this sharp and lip-smackingly tangy golden beer.

OUDE GEUZE VIEILLE

Oud Beersel, Beersel, Belgium

Type Lambic Strength 6%

• Saved from extinction by Frank Boon in 2005 – Oud Beersel procures wort from the nearby Brouwerij Boon which it then ferments in oak for up to three years to produce its lambic. Young and old lambics are then blended and refermented in bottle to produce this stunning gueuze. Lemon juice and wet hay mingle on the palate leading to a soft and subtle sourness that will leave you pining for one more sip.

PARTIZAN LEMON & THYME SAISON

Partizan Brewing, London, UK

Type Saison Strength 4%

• A relatively staple beer in a growing catalogue of Belgian-inspired farmhouse ales, the Lemon & Thyme Saison perfectly exhibits the nuanced, understated approach taken by Partizan. A straw-coloured, crisp and zesty beer which develops with time, its delicate acidity and herbal notes are shaped by a gently fruity yeast character. Deserves a place on the table beside seafood or cheese.

NICO

Orbit Beers, London, UK

Type Köln Style Ale Strength 4.8%

• It's decision to focus on German-style beers such as Altbier and Kölsch instead of modern IPA and pale ale means that South London's Orbit is one of the capital's most underrated breweries. Ignore them at your peril though, as you'll miss out on delightful beers such as Nico, a light and quaffable beer that fuses notes of red berry fruit and bready malts in homage to a classic beer style that originated in Cologne.

SUPPLICATION

Russian River Brewing Company, Santa Rosa, California, USA
Type American Sour Ale Strength 7%

• Although Russian River is perhaps best known for pale and hoppy beers, its sours are perhaps its truest expressions of its art. The Pinot Noir barrel-aged brown ale known as Supplication is one of the best sour beers being produced in the US, with ripe berry fruits at the fore, plus intense sour cherry notes from the fruit added to the barrel. Supplication is simply exceptional.

SAWMILL PILSNER

Sawmill, Matakana, New Zealand
Type Pilsner Strength 4.8%

• The New Zealand Motueka hop began its life as the humble Saaz, the southern hemisphere terroir adding tropical fruit qualities to its spicy, herbal character once relocated. This makes it ideal for lagers such as Sawmill's pilsner, where it's also joined by fellow Kiwi hops Riwaka and Nelson Sauvin, combining to conjure forth lemon and lime zest, zingy gooseberry and a spicy, peppery dry finish.

ABRICOT DU FERMIER

Side Project Brewing, Maplewood, Missouri, USA
Type Wild Ale Strength 8%

• Side Project was founded by Cory King while he was working at Perennial Artisan Ales. Happily, it's a fully-fledged brewery these days, which means he has time to devote to world-class beers like Abricot du Fermier. Made from a base of the brewery's Saison Fermier, it's aged with apricots in French oak wine barrels for more than a year.

PINEAPPLE SMOOSH

Søle Artisan Ales and Phantom Carriage Brewery, Easton, Pennsylvania and Gardena, California, USA
Type Milkshake Double IPA Strength 7.8%

• Made in collaboration with Phantom Carriage Brewery, the limited-edition Pineapple Smoosh is accomplished enough to convert dessert-beer antagonists. In the glass, it resembles liquid sunshine, and additions of lactose and vanilla have lent it a creamy mouthfeel. But it's the inspired choice of pineapple that makes this beer a tropical dream.

CELLAR DOOR

Stillwater Artisanal Ales, Baltimore, Maryland, USA
Type Saison Strength 6.6%

• According to luminaries like J.R.R. Tolkien, "cellar door" is an English phrase of particular beauty and euphony. Leave it to the high-browed folks at Stillwater to turn out a beer that embodies the delicacy, loveliness and balance of this phrase. A wheat beer that's accented with Sterling and Citra hops, as well as white sage, it's delicately grassy and citrusy, herbal, and lightly tart.

TOP 5

TOP 5 BEERS TO SHOW OFF WITH

We're not here to judge. We know occasionally you want to show-off, and why not. Whatever the occasion, whoever is visiting, there are some beers that drop jaws and knock people flat.

1. Tactical Nuclear Penguin (32%) - BrewDog

2. Cantillon Gueuze 100% Lambic Bio (5%) - Cantillon

3. Utopias (27%) - Sam Adam's

4. Chimay Grande Reserve (9%) - Chimay

5. Sorachi Ace (7.6%) - Brooklyn Brewery

TOP 5

TOP 5 BEERS TO MATURE

The desire to cellar beers and improve them over months and years has caught on in a big way in recent years, and many breweries know the value in providing a beer perfectly suited to ageing.

1. Fuller's Vintage Ale (8.5%) - Fuller's

2. Old Tom (8.5%) - Robinson's

3. Harvest Ale (11.5%) - JW Lees

4. White Shield (5.6%) - White Shield

5. Alaskan Smoked Porter (6.5%) - Alaskan Brewing Co

PACIFIC ALE

A Galaxy (beer) far, far away

Sometimes a beer manages to be not just an expression of a place, but also of a time. Stone & Wood's Pacific Ale, aside from being a beautifully thirst-quenching, clean and tropical-tasting beer, is also a product of a time when Australian craft beer and Australian hop development seemed to progress in unison.

Hops have been grown in Australia for over 150 years, and cross-breeding and growing European varieties in this climate has created very different hops, just like in the United States, New Zealand and South Africa. Galaxy was developed and grown as the Australian answer to hops like Citra and Simcoe, and in many ways, Galaxy surpasses them. With intense tropical notes, high alpha acids and overall oil content, it has the 'fairy dust' factor that brewers attribute to hops like Mosaic, which seem to invigorate any beer they are added to with near-magical qualities.

The pilot crop of Galaxy was released in 2008, just as fledgling craft brewery Stone & Wood was launching in Byron Bay. The brewers were looking for a hop that could convey the summertime sunshine vibe of the Northern Rivers region, and the citrus-and-passionfruit flavours of Galaxy were a perfect match.

A lightly hazy gold, Pacific Ale, uses Australian barley, wheat in its simple, gently sweet body, letting those super-juicy Galaxy hops take centre stage with aromas of pineapple and passion fruit. Galaxy's pink grapefruit notes are more prominent on the palate, with more passion fruit, lime and guava rounding out the fruit salad of flavours. Far from being unbalanced, Pacific Ale's finish is dry and bitter, making those fruit flavours all the more quenching at a sessionable 4.4% ABV.

The good news is that it's just as refreshing on a cold rainy day as it is on a hot beach in Australia.

the facts

Brewer Stone & Wood
Origin Byron Bay, Australia
Strength 4.4%
Type Pale Ale
Web www.stoneandwood.com.au
Temperature 6-8°C

TEGERNSEER HELL

Refined, elegant, unimprovable lager

Some beers are like giant monoliths, constructed from huge flavours stacked on top of each other. Others are more like gliders, require the most delicate balance, a light touch, and an almost fanatical pursuit of perfection. Tegernseer Hell glides.

The Herzogliches Bräustüberl Tegernsee ('Ducal Brewery of Tegernsee') traces its roots to a Benedictine abbey built in 746. The current brewery came much later, in 1675, and was eventually purchased by the House of Wittelsbach, which owns it to this day. When they say 'Ducal', they mean it: the brewery is owned and run by the Duchess Maria Anna of Bayern, daughter of the Duke of Bavaria.

Though Helles as a style didn't exist until 1894, Tegernseer Hell is the brewery's most famous beer, and has perhaps more a cult following than its main rival from Augustiner. Helles was first produced in response to the growing popularity of pale, hoppy Czech Pilsner in Bavaria. Bavarian brewers realised that they needed a pale beer of their own, or they would be swept aside. Helles is brewed to be different to a Pilsner: less hoppy, but with a more bready, easy-drinking body.

It pours the palest, brightest straw-gold colour, and its total, pure clarity is testament to its lengthy cold-conditioning time. Whilst light in colour, it's actually a full-bodied beer in some respects, as the brewers will try to extract as much protein as possible from the grain. Tegernseer Hell therefore has an almost paradoxical flavour – rich yet light, bready yet soft, sweet yet feathery. Its hop notes are gentle whispers of white pepper and lemon.

Tegernseer Hell's drinkability is such that the beer finishes much the way it begins: with you taking a sip of it. It is quite simply one of the most understated, elegant and precision-engineered beers in the world.

the facts

Brewer Herzogliches Bräustüberl Tegernsee
Origin Tegernsee, Bavaria, Germany
Strength 4.8%
Type Helles
Web www.braustuberl.de
Temperature 5-7°C

NINKASI

A superb Belgian-inspired beer/cider hybrid

If a single thing was to confirm the runaway success of The Wild Beer Co's saison, Ninkasi, it's that it was listed nationally by British supermarket chain Waitrose. It might not seem so out of the ordinary for this to happen to one of a particular brewery's most successful beers. However, when you consider that Ninkasi is a 9% Belgian-inspired beer infused with apple juice and refermented in the bottle with champagne yeast then the context of this huge achievement can be fully understood.

When The Wild Beer Co was established in Westcombe, Somerset, next door to the cheesemaker that also bears the village's name, one of its aims was to blur the line between wine and beer. It also wanted to prove that beer was just as good to pair with food as its grape-based cousin. To do this The Wild Beer Co use a vast range of ingredients outside of the norm, including foraged herbs and wild yeasts. Then they addressed the appearance of their packaging. In its smart 750ml bottle complete with white wax seal you could easily be forgiven for thinking Ninkasi was a bottle of wine instead of beer.

Ninkasi, named after the ancient Sumerian goddess of beer, appears the colour of pale straw with a busy, champagne-like head of foam produced as you pour. The nose is delicate, with aromas of straw, cut grass and apples but the taste is a little more complex, with a blend of wild yeasts and bacteria creating funky and complex flavours of just ripe berry fruit that mingles with the delicate flavour of apple as its lively effervescence prickles the tongue. Best enjoyed with an oversized, overripe slab of blue cheese.

the facts

Brewer The Wild Beer Company
Origin Somerset, UK
Strength 9%
Type Saison
Web www.wildbeerco.com
Temperature 8-10°C

GOSE

A lip-smacking cocktail of salt and sour

Westbrook Brewing Co was founded in 2011 by husband and wife team Edward and Morgan Westbrook, who got into craft beer like so many before them: homebrewing at university because it was cheap. Edward seemed to have a knack for flavour combinations though, and it shows in the beers that Westbrook now brew regularly, from juicy IPAs to a lemongrass and ginger Belgian Witbier.

Morgan's grandmother's German heritage inspired them to try out some traditional German styles, and their Gose is highly regarded by craft beer aficionados and style purists alike. Gose originated in the 16th century in the town of Goslar, taking its name from the river Gose, and was brewed with at least 50% malted wheat, coriander and salt. Industrialisation and the rise of pale lager marginalised Gose to obscurity by the 20th century. However, like many other regional styles, Gose benefitted from the thirst of the global craft beer movement for weird and wonderful brews. Westbrook's is a faithful take on what original Gose might have been like, with its flavours dialed up just a touch for the palates of beer geeks. Pouring a crisp, burnished gold, this beer practically shouts its aroma to you: citric freshness, just a little brine and some sweaty funk. As weird as that might sound, it's incredibly appetising, not unlike some natural wines.

After one sip, you'll understand, and you'll be hooked. The crispy texture tries to touch every part of your mouth – tangy, sharp lemon and exactly the right amount of salinity to contrast its sour notes.

It's easy to see how it might have been just the thing after a hard day of labour, sitting by the bank of the Gose.

the facts

Brewer Westbrook Brewing Co
Origin South Carolina, USA
Strength 4%
Type Gose
Web www.westbrookbrewing.com
Temperature 6-8°C

CANTILLON GUEUZE LAMBIC

Cantillon offers up tradition in a bottle

THE FACTS
Brewer Brasserie Cantillon
Origin Brussels, Belgium
Strength 5%
Type Sour Fruit Beer
Web www.cantillon.be
Temperature 8-10°C

The real skill of lambic brewing is not just the brewing itself, but also the blending of lambics aged one, two or three years to referment into gueuze. (Younger lambics have more residual sugar, providing more fuel for the secondary fermentation.) Cantillon's Gueuze Lambic is the beer most similar in appearance and character to champagne: a bright, hazy gold, sparkling and effervescent. The curious, musty sourness of lambic is the dominant aroma, similar to the smell in the brewery itself, but there are individual notes of apple, pear, honey, oak and bitter lemon.

Much of these same notes are found in the first sip, but the carbonation is very sharp, and if the beer is served too cold, many of these flavours will be lost. Allowing it to sit in the mouth for a second gives it a chance to tell its story – one that is years in the making. Juicy, acidic pear and rhubarb notes zing with flavour, but turn sour almost instantly, blossoming into mouth-puckering cider vinegar, apple skins and lemon rind.

The drying, acidic and elastically long finish is tinged with oak, vanilla and honeycomb. It stays fresh, despite all this weirdness, and the palate-stripping sourness, which to the unaccustomed seems so abhorrent at first, becomes so normal, desirable in fact, that other kinds of beer drunk seem flabby and clumsy by comparison. Gueuze's acidic tartness and sharp carbonation make it a wonderfully cutting and cleansing companion to sourdough bread, cured meats and pickles. It's a timeless classic of the beer world.

OUDE GUEUZE TILQUIN A L'ANCIENNE

Blend the best lambics and what do you get?

THE FACTS
Brewer Gueuzerie Tilquin
Origin Belgium
Strength 6.4%
Type Gueuze
Web www.gueuzerietilquin.be
Temperature 6-8°C

Gueuzerie Tilquin is the first new gueuzerie in over 15 years, and the only one in the region of Wallonia in Belgium. Tilquin has no brewhouse, instead buying in lambic beer brewed by a variety of lambic brewers and blending the beer for refermentation. The Gueuze a L'Ancienne is a blend of one, two and three-year-old lambics from Boon, Lindemans, Girardin and Cantillon. In fact, it's said that Tilquin is the only gueuzerie that Cantillon will sell their wort to.

Gueuze a L'Ancienne is a very pale, golden beer, unfiltered and unpasteurised, giving it an appetising haze beneath a collar of crisp, white bubbles. The sparkling character of the beer extends to its aroma, the tiny bubbles bursting with excitement to get up your nose. The aroma has pronounced cider vinegar, lemon, grape and gooseberry notes, with an unusual freshness and delicacy to its musty, barnyard aroma.

Gueuze as a style can be complex and confusingly deep, but Tilquin's has a remarkable clarity to each of its flavours, starting out with apples and pears, turning from sweet to sour, then ever so softly returning some juiciness to the palate before drying out with woody, bready depth. It's possibly the easiest gueuze to drink in the world, and a fantastic introduction to the style.

If you go to Belgium, you may be able to find the Tilquin Gueuze Draft, a 4.8% ABV version of the beer available on tap. It's even juicier, rounder and cleaner tasting. Both versions are wonderful summer beers.

HELL OR HIGH WATERMELON

21st Amendment Brewery, San Francisco, USA
Type Fruit Stout Strength 4.9%

• The kings of cool craft beer in cans, 21st Amendment's watermelon wheat beer is no exception, depicting Lady Liberty having a summer holiday at the Golden Gate Bridge. The beer itself is just as cool: an American wheat ale fermented a second time using watermelon puree. The effect is gentle, juicy and extremely refreshing, adding extra depth to the fruity sweetness in a wheat beer. A sensational summer seasonal beer.

PALATINE PILS

Suarez Family Brewery,
Hudson, New York State, USA
Type Pilsner Strength 5.2%

• Despite only establishing itself in 2016, New York State's Suarez Family Brewery is already one of the most respected new breweries in the US. This is mostly due to co-owner Dan Suarez's pedigree as a former brewer at Vermont's Hill Farmstead where he learned to craft immaculately balanced beers. Palatine Pils is a snappy, crispy little pilsner that's leading the trend for great craft lagers in the US.

VLIET

Threes Brewing, Brooklyn, New York, USA
Type Pilsner Strength 5.2%

• Threes, founded by three people and based at 333 Douglass Street, thankfully have more than three beers. In addition to a growing stable of equally brilliant lagers, IPAs and saisons, Threes is working on a variety of exciting barrel-aged and mixed fermentation projects. Vliet is still the best introduction to Threes' skill: an impeccably crafted, snappy pilsner that's bright, herbal and clean.

BEANN GULBAN

The White Hag Brewing Company,
Co. Sligo, Ireland
Type Sour/Wild Strength 7.5%

• As with Fraoch, the heather ale from Scotland's Williams Brothers, Beann Gulban from Ireland's The White Hag is a resurrection of a traditional heather ale. Beann Gulban completely forgoes hops in favour of heather and is fermented with wild yeasts to produce complexly tart and floral notes that are then accentuated by maturing in red wine barrels.

OUDE GUEUZE

Brouwerij Timmermans, Itterbeek, Belgium
Type Gueuze Strength 5.5%

• Revived by the brewery in 2009, Timmermans Oude Gueuze is the brewery's select blend of three-year-old lambic and young lambic, refermented in bottle. In 2015, it won gold in the Sour category of the World Beer Awards. When fresh, it has an outstandingly sharp acidity, like lime juice, and palate-cleansing crispness to its carbonation. Older bottles develop deeper, funky notes and become increasingly dry.

EXTRA VANILLA MILKSHAKE IPA

Tired Hands Brewing Company,
Pennsylvania, USA
Type Milkshake IPA Strength 7.5%

• Together with Omnipollo, Tired Hands has been instrumental in pioneering the Milkshake IPA sub-style: a creamy, hazy take on the IPA that's brewed with milk sugar and frequently has fruit added. In this iteration, the brew was conditioned atop a heaping quantity of vanilla beans. Mosaic and Citra hops add a pleasing bitterness, meanwhile, and prevent it from tasting one-note.

GEYSER GOSE

Two Roads Brewing Co. & Evil Twin Brewing,
USA/Denmark
Type Gose Strength 5.5%

• By nature, goses are lightly tart and distinctly saline – it's part of what makes the style so refreshing. But Geyser Gose takes the brininess to a new level. Made with a number of ingredients you'd likely find by the seaside, including Icelandic moss, kelp, birch-smoked sea salt, and other herbs, it sounds unusual but drinks like a dream.

10*

Únetický Pivovar, Únetice, Czech Republic
Type Pilsner Strength 3.8%

• This light pilsner-style beer, or svetly lezak as its known in its native Czech Republic, is a perfect example of why Bohemia is one of the best producers of lagers in the world. The malts in this lager evoke something similar to freshly baked bread, dripped with just a touch of butterscotch with a thick, white foaming head that's redolent with snappy, herbal Czech Saaz hops.

MEDORA

Wicked Weed Brewing,
Asheville, North Carolina, USA
Type Wild Ale Strength 6.6%

Medora begins its life as a tart blonde ale, before sitting in red wine barrels with blackberries and raspberries for nine months. As you might expect, it's got an amazing depth, showing off some rich, natural berry notes as well as a snappy sourness that stops it from ever being too sweet. It's a well-defined and carefully balanced American sour.

FILLE DE FERME

Wicked Weed Brewing, Asheville, North Carolina, USA
Type Farmhouse Ale Strength 4.2%

Its name – which translates to 'farm girl' – evokes a bucolic simplicity, but Fille de Ferme (right) is one complex beer. Inspired by Belgium's tradition for funky farmhouse ales, this lightly tart brew is fermented with Wicked Weed's house Brettanomyces culture, and blended with its Golden Sour Ale. The beer is then aged with wild honeysuckle flowers and orange peels in a foeder until it's perfectly zesty, floral, and complex.

FARMHOUSE PALE ALE

Oxbow Brewing Company, Maine, USA
Type Saison Strength 6%

It's not easy to balance farmhouse brewing tradition and modern craft beer boldness, but that's what Maine's Oxbow Brewing Company excel at. Its flagship Farmhouse Pale Ale exemplifies this with its even, rounded and delicate funk character. Yeast provides fruitiness, pilsner malt delivers the lightest grain flavour, and American hops offer zesty higher notes like an orchestra in perfect sync.

FOEDER CERISE

American Solera, Tulsa, Oklahoma, USA
Type Wild Ale Strength 5.5%

Started by one of the founders of Prairie Artisan Ales, American Solera launched in 2016 and was hailed by Ratebeer as the best new American brewery that same year. American Solera's patient approach to its craft is evident in beers like Foeder Cerise: a six-month foeder-aged cherry wild ale with spice, funk, sharp cherry notes and, above all, impeccable balance.

BOUNDARY TREE

Blackberry Farm Brewery,
Walland, Tennessee, USA
Type Saison Strength 6.3%

Blackberry Farm is an idyllic, luxury resort in the foothills of Tennessee's Smoky Mountains. Its on-site farmhouse brewery is also one of America's best and most authentic. From a wide range of impressive saisons, Boundary Tree (right) stands out for its poised hop profile of Citra and Hallertau Blanc, harmonising grape and citrus flavours with the sculpting influence of saison yeast.

TOP 5 BEERS FOR A BARBECUE

One of the most simple and life-affirming of pleasures, a beer at a barbecue needs to be easy-drinking, yet still have the flavour to match up to meat, fat, cheese and spicy sauces. Here are some beers that will make your next barbecue even better than the last one.

1. Camden Hells Lager (4.6%) – Camden Town Brewery
2. Doggie Style Pale Ale (5.5%) – Flying Dog
3. American Dream (4.6%) – Mikkeller
4. 5AM Saint (5%) – BrewDog
5. Ctrl Alt Delete (4.5%) – Nils Oscar

TOP 5 WEIRD BEERS

Let's face it, beers are getting weirder as brewers try to outdo each other in mad displays of creativity. Some deserve to exist as relics in a brewing museum, while others could be the seeds of established styles in years to come. But which is which?

1. Schnoodlepip (6.5%) – Wild Beer Co
2. Fraoch Heather Ale (5%) – Williams Bros
3. Brodie's Prime (4.9%) – Hawkshead
4. Sour Grapes (4.8%) – Lovibonds
5. Raging Bitch (8.3%) – Flying Dog

autumn

The shorter days bring cooler winds, carrying on them the auburn leaves that crunch underfoot as you make your way indoors from the diminishing sunshine. There's an increasing need to hunker down, gather richer, more warming foods, and comforting glasses of luscious, fuller-bodied beers. As the days turn amber, russet and maroon, so do the ales. A Belgian tripel wouldn't go amiss either, just to help take the edge off the chill in the air.

BREW BY NUMBERS
BBNº
01|01
SAISON
CITRA
5.7%
HANDCRAFTED IN LONDON
boulevard
BOULEVARD
BREWING CO.
KANSAS CITY
MO
BOULEVARD
BREWING CO.
SAISON
BRETT
RY-HOPPED FARMHOUSE ALE
WITH BRETTANOMYCES
MITED RELEASE
2017
1 PINT
9.4 FL OZ
ARVEY'S
BREWERY
SUSSEX
BEST
BITTER
ND OF FOUR LOCAL HOPS CREATES
A SUPERBLY BALANCED BITTER
LEWES·SUSSEX

CHISWICK BITTER

It may be low strength, but there's no doubting Chiswick's quality

It's rare to come across flavoursome bottled ale at just three and a half per cent, rarer still to see one describing itself as just 'bitter'. Chiswick Bitter's label offers a rather green and pleasant hop theme, suggesting that there must be something tasty going on inside. Chiswick is actually one of the finest hoppy, low-strength English bitters available, and better still, it's easy to find in supermarkets as well.

Chiswick is a very standard English Ale Amber on the paint chart of beer colours. The carbonation from a bottle is fairly high, and Chiswick sports a nice, thick head and is as clear as copper-coloured glass. One sniff transports you to a hop field in Kent, as all manner of floral, spicy whole-leaf goodness fills your nostrils. Northdown, Target, Challenger and Goldings hops are all used in Chiswick Bitter, and while the former three are hard to separate from the combined lemon-and-grapefruit aroma, Goldings' distinctive spicy note is easier to detect. It's a real bouquet for a lower-strength beer, and makes that first sip all the more appetising.

At first it struggles to find its feet, starting out soft, biscuity, lemony and tart, but this develops gradually into a complex and rounded English hop experience. At turns juicy, sharp, bitter, peppery and sweet, Chiswick really is a scrappy little session beer, giving out plenty of hop flavour for something so light and quaffable. The finish is pitch-perfect, delivering a crisp, wet smack of grassy, floral Goldings just in the right place, and it lasts for ages.

It's a classy, precisely-brewed beer, so something simple and well-seasoned is the best food match. Pub food like pork pies, sausage rolls and scotch eggs are perfect partners for Chiswick, allowing its crisp, peppery hops to enhance the savoury flavours without interfering too much. Fuller's have perfected something quite special here, so you have absolutely no excuse to settle for anything less.

the facts

Brewer Fuller's
Origin London, UK
Strength 3.5%
Type English Bitter
Web www.fullers.co.uk
Temperature 10-13°C

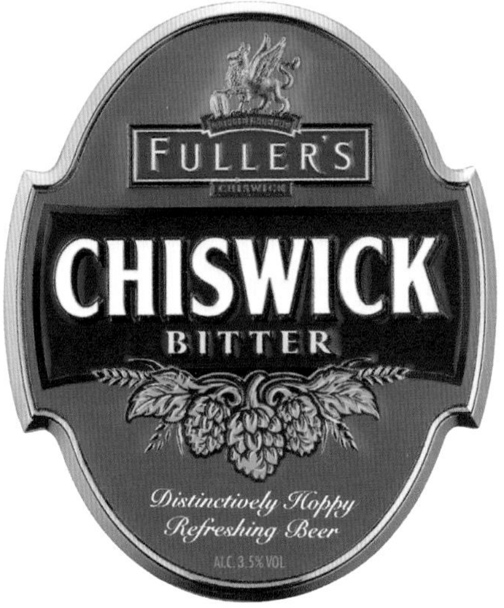

TANK 7

A modern American take on a classic Belgian saison

When you think of world-class Belgian-inspired saison you might not immediately think of Boulevard Brewing Company but by discounting them you'd be making a huge mistake.

Although the Kansas City, Missouri based brewery creates an accomplished range of beers that cover a wide variety of styles, such as 80-Acre Wheat and Single Wide IPA, its Tank 7 Saison is perhaps the largest jewel in its crown.

Whether it was fate or the talent of Boulevard's brewing team, or perhaps a combination of both, the perfect blend of time, ingredients and skill came together when this beer was first brewed. It just so happened that the first time it was produced this beer was fermented within fermentation tank number 7. Unsurprisingly the name stuck and so Tank 7 was born.

Tank 7 opens with aromas of freshly bailed hay, berry fruits and fresh citrus. There's a myriad of different flavours mingling together within this beer, with notes of grapefruit and redcurrant immediately coming to the fore – flavours produced by a combination of both a Belgian yeast strain and North American Hops. These eventually led to a grassy finish with hints of white pepper spice. Although complex, this beer is balanced, with all of these varied flavours working together, with one or the other never dominating this beer's character.

With its bold character and high 8.5% ABV there is an unmistakably American quality to this beer. However, despite its size there's a sense of balance and restraint to this beer that is unmistakably Belgian. As a result it's more than a fitting tribute to the beers that it was inspired by.

the facts

Brewer Boulevard Brewing Company
Origin Kansas City, Missouri, USA
Strength 8.5%
Type Saison
Web www.boulevard.com
Temperature 6-8°C

CITRA

A complex and fully contemporary take on the saison

It wasn't long ago that Bermondsey – an industrial, gritty stretch of South London – was well off most visitors' radars. But then came the breweries: once the likes of Brew By Numbers, The Kernel and Partizan moved into the neighbourhood's rumbling railway arches, Bermondsey transformed from an unlikely destination for casual flaneurs to the very heart of London's blossoming craft beer scene.

Much of Brew By Numbers' story has been similarly fortuitous. For instance: it was a twist of fate that brought together founders Tom Hutchings and Dave Seymour, who met while travelling in Southeast Asia, and who began homebrewing together upon their return to London. Their beery experiments quickly graduated to more advanced projects; by 2013, they had begun brewing in a railway arch on Enid Street, one of the main thoroughfares of the Bermondsey Beer Mile. In lieu of developing a core range, they settled on a system whereby each style was given its own number – 01 for saison, 05 for IPA, and so on – and then assigned a second number to denote the individual recipe.

Now one of the most versatile and innovative breweries in the city, if not the whole of the United Kingdom, Brew By Numbers is these days revered for its exceptional IPAs, its rich stouts, and its range of barrel-aged styles. But to really understand the brewery's ethos and early inspirations, begin with this superb saison.

In the inaugural 01|01, wheat is used as an addition, as well as aromatic Citra hops. The recipe's classic farmhouse origins, as well as its French ale yeast profile, are somewhat belied by the Citra, whose characteristic mango-driven fruit profile adds a contemporary twist. This was the beer – first described as a Hoppy Saison – that inspired Brew By Numbers' launch, and it tastes no less ravishing now.

the facts

Brewer Brew By Numbers
Origin London, UK
Strength 5.5%
Type Saison
Web www.brewbynumbers.com
Temperature 5-8°C

SAISON A LA PROVISION

An effortlessly graceful English farmhouse ale on a par with the best in the world

Burning Sky's founder Mark Tranter established his formidable brewing credentials as brewer and eventually Head Brewer at Dark Star from 1996 until 2013. One of the beers he was most proud of brewing during his tenure there was a Saison (far outside the brewery's comfort zone of hoppy pales and traditional bitter), so when Tranter struck out on his own, his love of Belgian styles heavily influenced the brewery he created.

Tranter's intention from the beginning was to authentically recreate the farmhouse beers of Belgium, but this would take months of experimenting, ageing, blending and work. Burning Sky's core range in the early days was composed of hoppy pale beers and four 'clean' saisons (released quarterly and named after each season). These beers paid wages and kept the lights on, until beers like Saison à la Provision, Saison Anniversaire, Monolith and Cuvée were released, to almost universal acclaim.

Based on the aged, stronger saisons that farmhouse brewers would have sent to local taverns (as opposed to the lighter, fresher ones consumed by the farm's workforce), Saison à la Provision undergoes a primary fermentation with saison yeast, before being fermented again with a blend of wild Brettanomyces strains and Lactobacillus (souring bacteria) in an oak foudre for three months.

Mostly noble hops and a small amount of Sorachi Ace give Saison à la Provision a light, peppery flavour, and a very mild vanilla and coconut character from the interplay between hops, yeast and oak. A gentle tartness lifts the flavours along with a fine, crisp carbonation, giving it a revitalising, almost zesty, dry finish.

Burning Sky have proven not just that elegant expressions of farmhouse brewing like Saison à la Provision can be made in the UK, but that they can also be the equal of the best examples brewed anywhere in the world.

the facts

Brewer Burning Sky Brewery
Origin Firle, East Sussex, UK
Strength 6.5%
Type Saison
Web www.burningskybeer.com
Temperature 6-8°C

HARVEY'S SUSSEX BEST

A benchmark for the classic Best Bitter style

In recent years Best Bitter has fallen somewhat out of favour with beer's new generation of drinkers. This is a shame, because it's a beer style that inspired would-be brewers from all over the world when they visited the UK before going on to start breweries of their own. If you ask any visiting brewer from outside the UK what inspired them to start making beer then 9 times out of 10 they will probably reply: "Harvey's Sussex Best."

It's hard to put your finger on what makes Harvey's Sussex Best just so tasty and so very drinkable. It might be the snap of earthy and fruity British hop varieties, it might be the gentle sweetness imbued by the Maris Otter malted barley, it might be the dry, mineral finish – or it might be something you can't quite put your finger on, a delicate complexity provided by Harvey's own unique house strain of yeast.

It's been said that after a few months a yeast strain which may or may not be a type of Brettanomyces, a yeast known to add fruity, funky flavours to beer, takes hold and changes the character of Harvey's beers such as Best. However, a cask of best will rarely last longer than a few hours, such is its popularity among its faithful, so it's not a quality that ever really gets the chance to get hold. Although if you wish to observe it more closely it can be found in a bottle of Harvey's imperial stout.

As tastes mature we could be on the verge of a Best Bitter revival here in the UK and we really hope that we are. There will always be time for heady DIPAs and big Imperial Stouts but when all's said and done, few things can top the experience of a session on Harvey's Best.

the facts

Brewer Harvey's Brewery
Origin Lewes, Sussex
Strength 4%
Type Best Bitter
Web www.harveys.org.uk
Temperature 8-10°C

ANCHOR STEAM BEER

A mongrel from America's oldest craft brewery

THE FACTS
Brewer Anchor Brewing Co
Origin San Francisco, United States
Strength 4.8%
Type Steam Beer/Californian common
Web www.anchorbrewing.com
Temperature 6-8°C

Anchor claim to be America's first craft beer brewery. The brewery traces its roots as far back as 1871. Its modern history began in 1965 with the brewery on the brink of financial ruin and closure. A graduate by the name of Fritz Maytag happened to be enjoying one of Anchor's beers when the barman told him it would be the last. Maytag did what any beer drinker would do in this situation – he bought the brewery.

Today, their beers stand as institutional benchmarks of the style but in the early days of Maytag's era they were cutting edge. Their Anchor Summer Beer, first brewed in 1984, was America's first wheat beer since Prohibition. Steam Beer was first brewed in 1971.

Steam Beer, also called California common, is unique to California. The beer is warm fermented at ale temperatures with lager yeast and is cold conditioned in shallow, open air vessels. The result is a hybrid of ale's flavour and lager's crispness. The closest comparison is a tawny bitter from the south of England (though admittedly that statement is a bit like saying that American football is a bit like rugby).

Steam Beer emits an orange glow and an initially lively head that soon fades. A quick mouthful snatched through the froth is satisfying and rewards you with a juicy, rounded bitter malt profile with a lilting taste of orange marmalade and cinnamon. The mellow flavour and crisp aftertaste make this a beer for all occasions.

ANNA

A simple, elegant beer that develops increasingly complexity with time

THE FACTS
Brewer Hill Farmstead Brewery
Origin Greensboro, Vermont, USA
Strength 6.5%
Type Saison
Web www.hillfarmstead.com
Temperature 8-10°C

Many beer enthusiasts consider Hill Farmstead to be the greatest brewery in the world. It's owner and founder Shaun Hill is often considered to be as understated as the delicate beers his brewery produces – but no less complex a character. Naming one brewery the 'best in the world' is difficult of course, as so many breweries are attempting to produce so many different qualities in their beers. However, one sip of a Hill Farm beer and you too might just be convinced.

The problem is actually getting hold of some to try in the first place. Many beer enthusiasts will happily beg, borrow or steal in order to get hold of Hill's beers. The easiest way to do this is to make the long drive to Greensboro, Vermont from a city such as Boston, Massachusetts or Portland, Maine. Once you arrive at the brewery, based in Hill's actual family farmstead you can buy beers to drink there and to take away – so make sure you've plenty of room in your car so you can take as much beer away with you as the brewery will allow.

Anna is a saison that takes its name from Hill's grandfather's sister. It makes up part of the brewery's 'ancestral series' where all of the beers are named after a member of the Hill dynasty. This Belgian-inspired beer features Vermont wildflower honey as an added ingredient, which in turn imbues a floral quality to this beer. Best savoured all on its own to appreciate the delicate complexity of dry and floral notes, Anna will only develop with age, as this unfiltered beer will continue to evolve long after it is packaged.

RED ROCKET ALE

Bear Republic Brewing Co, California USA
Type Red Ale **Strength** 6.8%

• This crimson-tinged mahogany beer has an aroma of caramel, roasted malt, pine, fresh bread and a little mango. The first sip screams malt and caramel sweetness. It sits heavily while a gradual rumble of piney, resinous hops roll across the tongue. A blast of roasted coffee signals the beginning of an imperial-stout-esque finish, full of red fruit and dark chocolate.

BREEZE

Affinity Brew Co, London, UK
Type Saison **Strength** 3.8%

• Despite being such a young brewery, Tottenham's Affinity Brew Co has quickly established itself as one to watch in the London brewing scene. Its flagship beer is a sessionable table saison called Breeze that's brewed with lime zest and coriander seed, flavours of which mix and mingle with a slightly funky, dry Belgian yeast character.

BROADSIDE

Adnams, Southwold UK
Type Bitter **Strength** 4.7% in cask, 6.3% in bottle

• Whether Adnams Broadside is better from cask or bottle is a pub debate that will never die. It's good in both servings, with cask lending it a creamy smooth body, while the bottled version is strong and, for some, has more flavour. They're actually different recipes, with the bottled being the original. It has a deep, ruby brown colour, brown sugar and dried fruit aromas. Broadside's big body wraps your tongue in a muscular hug and smothers it warmly with rich, malt loaf and toffee flavours.

HARVEST ALE

JW Lees, Manchester UK
Type Strong Ale/Barley Wine
Strength 11.5%

• A cult legend in its own right, Harvest Ale has been made by JW Lees since 1986. It is made from freshly harvested barley in autumn and released just prior to Christmas. Although pasteurised, it will mature in the bottle and is recommended for drinking fresh or ageing. The profile can vary from vintage to vintage and depending on when it is drunk, but common characteristics include sumptuous chocolate, sherry, dried fruits and spice flavours.

TRIBUTE

St Austell, Cornwall UK
Type Bitter **Strength** 4.2%

• Tribute is the best-selling beer from Cornwall's largest regional brewer. First brewed in 1999 to celebrate a total solar eclipse in Britain which was best seen from Cornwall, it is now brewed to celebrate any occasion. It pours a light, oaky brown with orange and spice aromas, leading to a gently spicy orange marmalade, cinnamon and toffee taste with a complex, bittersweet finish.

SAISON DE BRETTAVILLE

Almanac Beer Company, San Francisco, California, USA
Type Saison **Strength** 7.2%

• Almanac is famous for its oak-aged, farm-inspired ales. This complex, nuanced and delicious saison uses 12 different strains of Brettanomyces (wild yeast), before ageing the resulting beer in white wine barrels and dry-hopping it with Hallertau Blanc, Mandarina and Mosaic. It sounds complicated, but the funky notes from the yeast and barrels dovetail beautifully with the delicate citrus hop notes.

LITTLE BRETT

Allagash Brewing Company, Portland, Maine, USA
Type American Wild Ale **Strength** 4.8%

• If you like Allagash's famous White Ale then you'll love Little Brett. This beer is 100% fermented with Allagash's house strain of Brettanomyces before being graced with an addition of Mosaic hops. It's tart and funky up front, with hints of mango and pineapple rounded off with a dry finish and just a kiss of acidity.

SAISON SAUVIN

8 Wired Brewing, Warkworth, New Zealand
Type Saison **Strength** 7%

• If you love the tropical and grassy qualities locked away inside New Zealand Nelson Sauvin hops then look no further than Saison Sauvin from 8 Wired Brewing. Saison Sauvin explodes out of the glass with notes of passion fruit and gooseberry before being rounded out with funky Belgian yeast esters and a bone dry finish.

RUMPKIN

Avery Brewing Co, Boulder, Colorado, USA
Type Pumpkin Ale **Strength** 17.5%

• Rumpkin is a pumpkin ale of walloping intensity and heady, exhilarating strength. To make this seasonal brew, Avery produces a base of rich, spice-led pumpkin ale before transferring it to fresh rum barrels, which impart their molasses sweetness to the beer. Deep copper in the glass, Rumpkin offers a bouquet of pumpkin, gingerbread, clove, vanilla, toffee, and rye bread notes, plus a luscious, almost sticky mouthfeel.

LA (SAINT) JEAN

Brasserie Craig Allen, Plessis de Roye, France
Type Saison **Strength** 4.5%

• You wouldn't think that some of the best craft beers being produced in France were being done so by a Scot – however that means you won't have tried the excellent beers produced by Brasserie Craig Allen. La (Saint) Jean is a classic Belgian-style farmhouse ale that evokes aromas of cut grass that has been left in the sun to slowly dry, which mingle with the barnyard funk of Belgian yeast.

CWTCH

Tiny Rebel, Wales, UK
Type Amber Ale **Strength** 4.6%

• Tiny by name and tiny by nature, this Welsh superstar brewery can't keep up with the huge demand they receive, so their beers are available on a sort of revolving basis. Cwtch (pronounced 'kutch', the Welsh word for cuddle) is worth seeking out when it's next available. It is amber in colour, with a vibrant hoppy aroma, and lush citrus, pine and caramel on the taste. It gives more than the modest strength would suggest.

SAISON BRETT

Boulevard Brewing Company, Kansas City, Missouri, USA
Type Farmhouse Ale **Strength** 8.5%

• Tank 7 is the base for this limited-edition release. Dry hopped, bottle-conditioned with Brettanomyces, and aged for a minimum of three months, Saison Brett offers a beautiful balance of honeyed sweetness and pleasing bitterness. On the palate, the beer offers a complex array of citrus, fruit, and vinous characteristics, which evolve into a spicy and off-dry finish.

D'ETRE

Boundary Brewing Cooperative, Belfast, Northern Ireland, UK
Type Saison **Strength** Varies

• Belfast's Boundary Brewing Cooperative has quickly built a reputation on the back of its pale ales and stouts. However, its barrel-ageing project is where head brewer Matthew Dick's true passion lies. D'être is a summation of his ambition, an ever-changing Saison that lets him push the boundaries of his creativity, whether it's "hopped up the wazoo" or laden with fresh fruit.

BATHAMS BEST BITTER

Bathams Brewery, Brierley Hill, West Midlands, UK
Type Best Bitter **Strength** 4.3%

• Some beers might be traditional, others might be the object of a cult following, but few can boast to be both. Only available locally to the brewery, 'The Batham's' is the definitive Black Country bitter, balancing a honeyed, bready body with peppery, leafy English hop character and finishing with a session-beer dryness.

HOP ROD RYE

Bear Republic Brewing Company, Healdsburg, California, USA
Type Rye IPA **Strength** 8%

• Hop Rod Rye is brewed with 18% rye malt – enough to impart the classic rye profile of spiciness and crisp-edged dryness to the brew. To match the rye's intensity, as well as the caramel sweetness provided by the barley malt, the brewery is generous with its hops. The end result boasts an aroma of sugared lemon and piney bitterness on the palate.

XXXB

Batemans, Wainfleet, Linconcolnshire, UK
Type Best Bitter **Strength** 4.8%

• Lincolnshire's Batemans Brewery is perhaps best known for its XB bitter, but those in the know will seek out its stronger, richer cousin, XXXB. This copper coloured beer is hopped with both Kentish and Styrian Goldings that add earthy and peppery qualities to a backbone of biscuit malt and vinous berry fruits before leading to a bitter finish.

EFFRA ALE

Brixton Brewery, Brixton, London, UK
Type American Amber Ale **Strength** 4.5%

• Named after an underground river flowing beneath Brixton in south London, Effra Ale takes its cues from both hoppy American amber ales and malt-forward English cask ales. Pine and citrus notes from American hops merge with rich, soft fruitcake flavours, until you can't tell where the hops begin and the malt ends. An understated, well-made session beer.

THE LOW END

Casey Brewing & Blending,
Glenwood Springs, Colorado, USA
Type Saison **Strength** 4.5%%

• To visit Casey Brewing & Blending you'll need to travel way up into the Rocky Mountains, to a town called Glenwood Springs. Here you'll find a modestly sized brewery filled with oak barrels. It's here owner Troy Casey produces some of the best sour beers in the world. One of these beers is The Low End, a lightly tart Saison that puckers the palate with notes of lemon juice and freshly bailed hay.

ANIANISH DRY HOPPED CUVEE

De Garde Brewing, Tillamook, Oregon, USA
Type Wild Ale **Strength** 5.2%

• Many breweries experiment with wild yeast—but few US-based breweries are quite so wild as De Garde. Based in coastal Oregon, De Garde eschews laboratory-cultured yeast; instead, its wort is exposed to the region's diverse microflora via coolships. As with all of De Garde's beers, the Anianish Dry Hopped Cuvée is aged in oak barrels. It's bright with stone fruit and lychee notes, constructed on an armature of hop bitterness.

LORD NELSON

Elusive Brewing, Berkshire, UK
Type Saison **Strength** 6.5%

• Elusive Brewing announced itself to the UK beer market by launching with this collaboration brew with London's Weird Beard Brew Co. Elusive owner and head brewer Andy Parker has a love for New Zealand Nelson Sauvin Hops and he uses them in this Belgian style farmhouse ale to great effect. Expect notes of passion fruit, lychee and gooseberry combined with a Belgianesque yeasty funk.

OUD BRUIN

Brouwerij t'Verzet, Anzegem, Belgium
Type Oud Bruin **Strength** 6%

• For a brewery that's so young, Belgium's Brouwerij t'Verzet crafts beers that demonstrate an incredible level of maturity. Its flagship Oud Bruin, this oak-aged sour red beer brings this classic Belgian style into the modern era. Oak and sweet raspberry jam is on the nose and to taste you find sour cherries and cranberries with a touch of green apple acidity leading to an oaky, dry finish.

COLORADO WILDSAGE

Crooked Stave Artisans Beer Project,
Denver, Colorado, USA
Type Saison **Strength** 7.2%

• Crooked Stave began life in Fort Collins before relocating to Denver, but Colorado WildSage is designed to evoke more untamed climes of this mountainous state. Brewed with locally picked white sage and lemongrass, this funky saison offers up plenty of lemony tartness, as well as a Brettanomyces-led complexity. Rather than tasting medicinal or astringent, its sage profile is fresh and herbaceous.

SAISON RUSTIQUE

Brasserie Dunham,
Dunham, Quebec, Canada
Type Saison **Strength** 6%

• Once just a small brewpub in rural Canada, Quebec's Brasserie Dunham has become one of the leading producers of innovative farmhouse ales in North America. The bright gold Saison Rustique is bursting with distinctive wild yeast notes of fruit, funk and spice. Younger bottles have a little zesty hop character; older ones have more funk, depth and crispiness.

NIGHT OWL

Elysian Brewing Company, Seattle, USA
Type Pumpkin Ale **Strength** 6.7%

• Elysian's seasonal Night Owl, one of several examples of the style that the brewery bottles each year, remains one of the finest in its category. Conditioned with a clutch of autumnal spices (ginger, cinnamon, nutmeg, cloves, and allspice), this medium-bodied pumpkin ale pours a pretty shade of copper, and offers up caramel and rich pumpkin pie on the palate.

SAISON
Brasserie Fantôme, Soy, Belgium
Type Saison **Strength** 8%

• Fantôme is one of the world's most unusual and eccentric breweries. Brewing on outdated equipment, frequently with recipes from memory, Dany Prignon has developed a global cult following for his extremely varied takes on farmhouse ales. His (anything but) 'regular' Saison is perhaps the best place to begin, with the signature musty, funky aroma and crisp, dry texture associated with Fantôme.

BLACK HOPS
Golden Triangle, Norwich, UK
Type Black IPA **Strength** 4.6%

• Norfolk's Golden Triangle is one of those small, regional British breweries that demonstrate the diversity amongst the UK's traditional microbreweries. Its Black Hops, which they call an 'India Black Ale' is much lighter on the palate than its dark appearance suggests. Expect notes of liquorice that mingle with a hint of black treacle sweetness that combine with a satisfyingly bitter finish to make this a very refreshing beer to be enjoyed by the pint.

FULLER'S ESB
Fuller's, London UK
Type Bitter **Strength** 5.5% in cask, 5.9% in bottle

• Fuller's launched a new style in 1971 when they made their seasonal winter brew a permanent addition and named it Extra Special Bitter. ESB is made with four varieties of English hop for a deeply British taste. It has a polished mahogany colour and full body, with complex aromas of toffee, orange, lemon and lime marmalade and subtle hedgerow woodiness. The taste is equally worthy of the smell, with lashings of marmalade and biscuits leading to a peppery hop finish.

BLACK SHEEP BEST BITTER
Black Sheep Brewery, Yorkshire UK
Type Bitter **Strength** 3.8%

• When Paul Theakston, of the famous Theakston brewing family, fell out with his family he founded his own brewery in 1992. The Black Sheep name naturally followed. Black Sheep Best Bitter is amber in colour with a tart, hoppy aroma. On the palate it has chewy caramel, citrus and pepper notes. The body is well carbonated and combines well with a dry, bitter finish that refreshes and cleanses the palate, making it suited to red meats and salty cheese. Available from supermarkets, off-licences and online retailers.

TOP 5

TOP 5 LOW STRENGTH BEERS

Sometimes you need to wet the whistle without going off into the deep end. Weak no longer means bland, and low strength beers slot in nicely as the lunch time pint, if you have to drive or to take the edge off a long drinking session.

1 Table Beer (3%)
- The Kernel

2 Wild Swan (3.5%)
- Thornbridge

3 Kriek (3.5%)
- Lindemans

4 Sole Star (2.8%)
- Adnam's

5 Black Cat (3.5%)
- Moorhouse's

TOP 5

TOP 5 CLASSIC BEERS

You can't beat a good classic beer and even when modern tastes move on, it's good to appreciate where it all began.

1 Summer Lightning (5%)
- Hop Back Brewery

2 Foreign Export Stout (7.5%) - Guinness

3 Pilsner Urquell(4.4%)
- Plzensky Prazdroj

4 Landlord (4.3%)
- Timothy Taylor

5 Sierra Nevada Pale Ale (5.6%)
- Sierra Nevada

LA FOLIE

Sour notes of forest fruits with a tannic finish

New Belgium Brewing, the fourth largest craft brewer in the United States according to the Brewers Association, is perhaps best known for its Belgian-inspired amber ale, Fat Tire. However, there's far more to this Colorado-based brewery than meets the eye and should you get a chance to take a tour of its Fort Collins facility then you'll soon learn why.

Once you've been taken past the giant steel vessels where the brewing process begins you're led into the sour beer production room – the largest of its kind in the US. This room is known at the brewery as the 'Foudre Forest' as it's home to no less than 64 oak vats, known as foudres, some of which are up to 200 hectolitres in size. It's here that New Belgium's base sour beers, 'Felix' and 'Oscar' are aged in the wood for up to two years before blending into a finished product.

La Folie is the Colorado brewery's flagship sour beer and it's released annually. This dark and sour beer is composed of a blend of Oscar from different vats so as to produce the perfect balance of tartness, sweetness and acidity, much like in winemaking. New Belgium's master blender Lauren Salazar keeps meticulously detailed notes of how the beer in each foudre is progressing, before pulling samples and continuously tasting so that each year's blend is as good as the last.

This beer is inspired by the traditional Oud Bruins of Belgium, such as Rodenbach Grand Cru and the flavour profile is similar, although turned up a notch or two as the Americans like to do. Expect sour flavours of forest fruits coupled with a bright and moreish acidity before leading to a dry and tannic finish.

the facts

Brewer New Belgium Brewing
Origin Fort Collins, Colorado, USA
Strength 7%
Type American Sour Ale
Web www.newbelgium.com
Temperature 8-10°C

WESTMALLE TRIPEL

Time slows down when you drink Westmalle Tripel

The Westmalle Abbey has been brewing since the 1830s. Initially the beer they produced was to quench the thirsts of the monastery brothers, then in the 1860s their commercial brewing experience took off when they sought to raise funds for overseas aid. From small beginnings, Westmalle has come on to be the second largest producer of the Trappist breweries. More fittingly for the brewery that produces the benchmark tripel ale, Westmalle first introduced the terms dubbel and tripel which have gone on to define Trappist and Belgian beers. Dubbels are darker and fruity, around 6-7% ABV, while tripels are stronger but paler in colour, and typically come with more hop, spice and citrus characteristics.

Westmalle Tripel is a beautiful, pale gold beer, with some haze if the yeast sediment is disturbed, and a brief flash of white head. The aroma is rich and soothing, with a muscular booze note kept calm by sweet candi sugar, toffee and fresh yeast notes.

The body is thick, almost syrup-like, and is probably made dense by the complex flavour profile it manages to pack in rather than the 9.5% ABV strength. The ale offers up an ever-changing flavour chart of honeycomb, tangy earth notes and toasted white bread in the foretaste. Banana and cherries soaked in brandy take up the midsection, followed by a warm, dry spice finish that's also sugar sweet on occasion.

It's near impossible to convey how excellent Westmalle Tripel is. Terms like 'liquid gold' and 'amber nectar' can seem trite and hackneyed, but in reality those words are fraudulent – if applied to any other beer. Westmalle Tripel owns them, spiritually if not legally. Time slows down when you're having this peerless Belgian Tripel.

the facts

Brewer Westmalle Abbey Brewery
Origin Westmalle, Belgium
Strength 9.5%
Type Belgian Tripel
Web www.trappistwestmalle.be
Temperature 12-16°C

CHIMAY BLEU

The strongest Chimay is perfect for sitting back and winding down with

Chimay is one of the most well-known and widely sold Belgian trappist ales. There are three expressions in the Chimay range and at 9% ABV Chimay Blue is the strongest. Then there's Chimay Rouge, a Belgian bruin (brown) ale, 7% ABV, and the Chimay Blanche, a Triple at 8% ABV. They're also available in larger Grand Cru bottles and take on different names, Premiere for Rouge, Cinq Cents for Blanche and Grande Reserve for Bleu.

Chimay Bleu has a dark, solid brown colour, tinged with mahogany highlights around the edges of the glass. It's recommended to drink all Chimay beers from a chalice or goblet: the wide-mouth of a chalice glass lets the pressure of the Belgian ale ease off, allowing the fragrant smell of red wine, oak, apricot and nutmeg to come through more easily. There's also a palpable sense of strength in the aroma – which is hardly surprising.

From the first mouthful there's staggering depth. A sharp, bitter foretaste surges forward, lasting for a few fleeting seconds. Then fruity, plummy port-wine flavours rise up, bolstered by a woody note which finally falls back to allow a candied sugar-rush to ride through. In the final moments a spike of sudden pepper lends a bitter note to the finish. A deliciously satisfying warmth hugs the back of the throat.

Chimay Bleu constantly develops, particularly as it gradually warms up, taking on spiced rum qualities of wood, molasses, vanilla and nutmeg. Towards the end it becomes even boozier on the nose, the bitterness receding from the taste until pepper and caramel sweetness tug back and forth on the palate.

This is one for hazy summer evenings with friends in a darkening beer garden, or winter nights with a good book and the comfort of a cosy chair. Chimay Bleu also works well as a digestif at the end of a big meal, served alongside strong, blue cheese.

the facts

Brewer Chimay, Scourmont Abbey
Origin Hainaut, Belgium
Strength 9%
Type Trappist Ale
Web www.chimay.com
Temperature 12-16°C

TRAPPISTES ROCHEFORT 10

A luxuriously decadent benchmark of the Belgian quadruple style

Faithful to the Trappist tradition of specialising in a few, select beers, the monks of the Abbaye St. Remy near Rochefort only make three beers: the 6, 8 and 10. Unlike the world of whisky, this isn't a reference to the number of years these beers have been aged. The numbers relate to Belgian degrees, a method of measuring the sugar in the beer before it's fermented. The higher the number, the greater the volume of sugar and the more the yeast can convert to alcohol.

The beers increase in strength and depth as they increase in scale, with Rochefort 10 being the ultimate expression of the range. It is a rich, deep brown colour that shines with a buff polish. It begins with a pretty generous off-white head that slowly dims down to a thin, foamy layer. Given the 11.3% ABV, the aroma is initially heavy with rich red wine, bonfire toffee and leather notes. Once the alcohol starts to dissipate and the glass warms up in your hand, the aroma shifts to dried fruit notes of fig and plum before finally settling on almond and caramel.

The taste goes through a similar evolution, practically knocking you flat with its first spicy, warming sip, like mulled red wine with a bottomless depth. The second sip gives crystallised fruits dusted with cinnamon, clove and nutmeg. It's at the point when the aroma settles on almond that the taste reaches equilibrium, rewarding patient drinkers with decadent rum-like notes of leather, cocoa, vanilla and gentle spice. The finish is bittersweet, oaky and genuinely dry – as soon as the mouthful is swallowed the tongue shrivels up in protest and cries out for more of this Belgian elixir.

Whatever else changes, the body of this drink is always slick and boozy and guaranteed to banish a chill. Savour Rochefort 10 along with a steak coated in blue cheese sauce on a cold evening.

the facts

Brewer Abbaye St. Remy
Origin Rochefort, Belgium
Strength 11.3%
Type Trappist Ale
Web www.trappistes-rochefort.com
Temperature 12-16°C

RODENBACH GRAND CRU

A dark, luxuriously flavoursome aged beer

THE FACTS
Brewer Rodenbach Brewery
Origin Roeselare, Belgium
Strength 6%
Type Red Ale
Web www.rodenbach.be
Temperature 12-16°C

The Rodenbach Brewery only really make one type of beer, the definitive Flanders Red ale that remains a world classic more than a hundred years after it was first brewed. The brewery was found in the early 1800s by the four Rodenbach brothers, and remained under family ownership until 1998 when it was bought by Palm Breweries.

Rodenbach's aged beer is conditioned for four months after primary fermentation and is then transferred to one of 300 giant wooden vats, some of which can hold 65,000 litres. It is in these vats that the beer takes on its tart, sour, acetic qualities as it matures for up to two years. The 'ordinary' Rodenbach uses 75% freshly brewed beer and 25% of the matured beer. It's a lovely, sweet, warming fruity and tart beer, but pales in comparison to the Grand Cru, which uses 67% aged beer to 33% fresh beer. A rich, vinous depth of flavour defines this very dark red beer, and its aroma is a magnificent blend of grapefruit, cherry jam and malty, chocolatey notes.

The beer's flavour depends a great deal on its temperature; too cool and it's a very fresh, fruity-tasting dark ale; but at a cellar temperature or slightly warmer, it blossoms with woody, vanilla and tart cherry notes that are deep, lasting and just sour enough to pucker the mouth. It is this perfect level of sourness that makes Rodenbach Grand Cru so hugely refreshing, balancing the heavy, stone fruit sweetness majestically.

For a food pairing, it needs a dish just as rich to match, fatty meats like duck are perfect.

STRAFFE HENDRIK QUADRUPEL

The quad that everyone can get along with

THE FACTS
Brewer Brouwerij de Halve Maan
Origin Bruges, Belgium
Strength 11%
Type Quadruple
Web www.halvemaan.be
Temperature 12-16°C

Brouwerij de Halve Maan is the only brewery to brew and package its beers within the city of Bruges, and concentrates on three main beers: its Bruges Zot Blonde, a Bruges Zot Bruin and Straffe Hendrik Tripel. Recently, de Halve Maan have ventured into the brewing of a quadrupel under the Straffe Hendrik branding, available in either 330ml or 750ml bottles.

Full-bodied and syrupy sweet, with a moreish balance of toffee, chocolate and coffee notes, Straffe Hendrik Quadrupel should be the quad that almost everyone can get along with. It pours darker than many Trappist and abbey quads, a rich, dark brown with a smooth, off-white head. It has a warming and fruity aroma of plums, stewed fruit pudding, dark rum, raisins and melting milk chocolate. It's quite an intoxicating nose, but just as appealing and seemingly accessible as a particularly aromatic porter or stout. There's no sense of superhuman strength. Yet.

However, once it gets a chance to go to work on your tongue, it proves to be a very thick beer, its texture and sweetness at first like fruitcake or rumcake. Vinous, sherry-like booziness rides through it like an elephant, but this is balanced by a syrupy cherry sauce flavour. Underneath all this are chunks of fruit and nut chocolate, more booze and then, most surprising of all, a silky finish of more tart cherries and chocolate.

Strong cheeses, blue and crumbly ones in particular, alongside a big slab of fruitcake is the ideal match to this decadent and loveable take on a quad. The beer has the strength and fruitiness to slap down any perfumed, funky notes from the cheese, whilst its syrupy, finely-carbonated, chocolatey body is the perfect partner to sticky fruitcake.

WESTMALLE DUBBEL

Westmalle Abbey Brewery, Belgium
Type Belgian Dubbel **Strength** 7%

• The good folk at Westmalle brew three famous beers: the Tripel, the Dubbel and the Extra. The Extra can't be had on the market – it's only available at the Abbey and is exclusively for the monks and visitors – while Tripel and Dubbel are the second most best-selling of the Trappist beers. Westmalle Dubbel is dark in appearance with a complex chocolate and dried fruit aroma; this comes through in the taste with a sweet, malty finish.

TRIPEL KARMELIET

Bosteels Brewery, Buggenhout, Belgium
Type Belgian Tripel **Strength** 8%

• Tripel by name, triple by nature, Karmeliet is made with three grains: barley, wheat and oats. Although first produced in 1996, this Belgian golden ale is made according to a recipe designed by Carmelite monks in 1679. Perhaps due to the wheat and oats, which tend to be uncommon in Belgian ales, Karmeliet has even more spicy notes and a much drier astringency accompanying the banana esters, dried fruits and deep malt sweetness.

LONDON ALT

Mondo Brewing Company, London, UK
Type Altbier **Strength** 4.8%

• Mondo Brewing Company's London Alt is a malt-based sanctuary in a hostile world of hazy, hoppy styles. Hop forward pales are delicious but sometimes you just want a toasty, crispy little beer with a smack of noble hob bitterness and a dry, fruitcake finish. For those times, reach for Mondo's London Alt and when that's gone reach for another.

HAIKU DE SAISON

Monkish Brewing Co, California, USA
Type Saison **Strength** 6.3%

• Before becoming an accomplished producer of the most on-trend hazy IPAs, Monkish built its reputation on multi-faceted and deeply complex farmhouse beers. Haiku de Saison is aged in oak foudres (vats) formerly used to make white wine, so you can expect layers of fruity, vinous and earthy notes in this beer, ably sculpted by a mixed culture of wild yeasts and souring bacteria.

FAT TIRE

New Belgium, Fort Collins, Colorado, USA
Type Amber Ale **Strength** 5.2%

• Fat Tire is a beer for those times when you're not sure what you want to drink and for this reason it makes it into this book. Its biscuit and oatmeal character provide comfort and shelter when presented with a beer list that looks like an encyclopedia and its delicate, dry biscuit malt and snappy herbal hop finish means that if you still haven't decided by the time you finish your pint, there's always more Fat Tire.

APEX PREDATOR

Off Color Brewing, Chicago, Illinois, USA
Type Farmhouse Ale **Strength** 6.5%

• If there's a single brewery that represents the idiosyncratic diversity of Chicago's brewing scene then surely it's Off Color Brewing. Off Color specialise by producing unusual ferments with their house yeast strain and their farmhouse ale, Apex Predator, is their flagship. To taste this beer you'll find pithy pineapple, fresh hay, barnyard funk and a tartness not unlike the one you'd find in a great piece of blue cheese. Curiously delicious.

CUVEE ADINA

Partizan Brewing, London, UK
Type Sour/Wild Ale **Strength** 5.5%

• Partizan are well loved within the London beer scene, but their small batch, annually released Cuvée series evades all but the most ardent fans of their beer. This bright and tartly acidic saison is blended with a small amount of lambic from Belgium's Girardin. To taste you'll detect plenty of lemon juice and hay, with a suitably punchy amount of funk from wild yeasts. If you can hang on to it, this beer should age beautifully.

DUCHESSE DE BOURGOGNE

Brouwerij Verhaeghe, Vichte, Belgium
Type Belgian Trappist **Strength** 6.2%

• Showing a more spiky side to Flemish reds and oud bruins, this sharp and sour example from Verhaeghe has a very clear cider vinegar note in its rich, boozy, stewed fruit and toffee pudding aroma, but don't be put off. This beer is invigoratingly sour in just the right places, livening up its oak-aged, syrupy fruit flavours with tart notes of pear, currants and cranberries.

1

2

3

BRASSIERIE DE LA SENNE JAMBE DE BOIS (1)

Brasserie de la Senne, Brussels, Belgium
Type Belgian Tripel **Strength** 8%

• This orangey and peppery tripel is named after the one-legged Belgian revolutionary on its label, Jean-Joseph Charlier (Jambe de Bois means 'wooden leg'), who was a major figure in the successful Belgian Revolution of 1830. The tripel named in his honour has a full, round and berry-sweet hop profile, laid over a full-bodied, biscuity and spicy base. There are even notes of garden herbs and grapefruit in its complex finish.

DELIRIUM TREMENS (2)

Brouwerij Huyghe, Melle, Belgium
Type Belgian Ale **Strength** 8.5%

• Delirium is a world-famous strong Belgian ale, whose bottle is adorned by pink elephants and various hallucinations. Whilst its name refers to the 'trembling madness' of withdrawal from alcohol addiction, it's not really dangerous at all. The earthy, yeasty notes are woven into a tangle of lemon rinds, apple skins and grapes. A slightly fig-like tartness is blended into bananas and caramel, building to a sweet and astringent finish.

PAUWEL KWAK

Bosteels Brewery, Buggenhout, Belgium
Type Belgian ale **Strength** 8%

• Pauwel Kwak is traditionally served in a fluted glass with a rounded base and it needs its own wooden 'shoke' for support. This design goes back to a time in Belgium when coach drivers couldn't leave their carriages unattended. They would stop beside De Hoorn Tavern and Fat Paul, the landlord, would hand them a glass which slotted onto the side of their carriage. Pauwel Kwak has a sweet, caramel and malt flavour along with banana, vanilla and a dry, toasted finish.

RYEWAY TO HEAVEN (3)

Revolution Brewing, Chicago, Illinois
Type Imperial Rye Ale **Strength** 14.5%

• Whether you take your rye in beer or whisky form, Revolution's Ryeway to Heaven delivers the goods. A generous amount of rye is used in the mash, which lends this beer spice and complexity; time spent ageing in rye whisky barrels, meanwhile, imparts a perfume of vanilla, brown sugar, dark fruit and caramel. Its richness of body – and heady alcohol content – make it perfect for autumn and winter evenings.

TOP 5 BEERS FOR SHARING

Beers that are sold in larger bottle sizes are great for sharing with friends, especially if they are particularly high in strength or are suited to certain foods. Whether you are planning to enjoy them with a meal, or just on their own, these beers are perfect for sharing.

1. Estrella Damm Inedit (4.8% – 750ml) – Estrella Damm

2. Hardcore IPA (9.2% – 660ml) – BrewDog

3. Rose de Gambrinus (5% – 750ml) – Brasserie Cantillon

4. Speedway Stout (12% – 750ml) – Alesmith

5. Hitachino Nest White Ale (5.5% – 720ml) – Kiuchi Brewery

TOP 5 SUPERMARKET OWN BRAND BEERS

Forget about those value cans of 2% lager. Supermarkets now have beers brewed for them under contract by some of the UK's best breweries, making it even easier to buy good quality beer for less.

1. M&S Citra IPA (4.9%) – Oakham Ales

2. Sainsbury's Taste the Difference Scottish Craft Lager (4.1%) – Harviestoun

3. M&S Southwold Summer IPA (6.8%) – Adnams

4. Waitrose Duchy Originals Old Ruby Ale (5%) – Wychwood

5. Tesco Finest Traditional Porter (6%) – Harviestoun

ORVAL

An accessible heavyweight of the Belgian beer scene

They only make one beer at the Abbey of our Lady of Orval. The Cistercian monks focus all of their energies on crafting Orval, which undergoes three stages of fermentation. The first stage is a standard fermentation process with ale yeast; after that they add several more different yeasts to the batch, including Brettanomyces (or brett for short), a wild yeast. This yeast eats up all of the sugars in the beer, so at the bottling stage the original yeast and extra brewing sugar is added to kick-off the third fermentation.

Orval has a deep, orange hue, like the soft glow from an open fireplace. There's a good level of carbonation, helping to sustain a very generous head of brilliant white foam which stays right through to the end.

The wild yeast is the star attraction of Orval, defining the aroma and taste in a uniquely Belgian way. Few breweries outside of Belgium work with brett yeast, and while more breweries are starting to experiment with it, the Cistercian monks at Orval continue to work it expertly as they have done since 1931.

Sour, lactic aromas of lemon, marmalade and hints of cider vinegar can surprise the unwary, but it really is a fantastic smell which is quickly appreciated. It's sharp and earthy in equal measure. Belgian sour beers can be an acquired taste, the sharp, acidic flavours overloading tastebuds that are used to crisp lagers or hoppy ales. But Orval is a good introduction to the lambic style. It's a quick hit-and-run rather than a full-on collision, the sharp, lemon notes soon turning into tangy, bittersweet orange, then reassuring plum flavours, cherries and dried apricots.
The long, dry finish ends on a final earthy, acidic hit.

The bottle carries the 'bottled on date', which is always interesting to note. Especially since Orval's character develops over time, starting fresher and hoppier; at six months it has the above characteristics, and a year down the line the yeast is the main player, with more dried fruit flavours.

the facts

Brewer Orval Abbey Brewery
Origin Villers-devant-Orval, Belgium
Strength 6.2%
Type Trappist Ale
Web www.orval.be
Temperature 12-14°C

THE LEGEND

Orval beer begins with a legend that dates back to the 11th century. After journeying from Italy, a small group of monks chose to build their monastery amid the peaceful woodlands of the Ardennes. They soon received a powerful visitor: Countess Matilda of Tuscany, who was still grieving for her late husband. Desiring a moment of quiet contemplation to carry out her mourning, the Countess took to the serenity of the woodland and perched beside a lake. Her tranquillity was shattered, however, when her wedding band fell into the water. She fell to her knees in despair and prayed to God for help. Then, as if by divine intervention, a trout rose up from the water, the ring offered up in its mouth. Countess Matilda wept with joy, declaring that "Truly this place is a Val d'Or!"

Val d'Or meant Golden Valley, and from that expression Orval is derived. And it is said Countess Matilda bequeathed money to the monks to expand their monastery.

DUVEL

A devilish introduction to strong yet quaffable Belgian beer

This classic Belgian strong golden ale became commonplace outside of Belgium a long time ago, but despite its commercial popularity, it remains an enjoyable and deceptively strong treat. It is still often named by people as being the tempting introduction to strong and interesting beer – fitting given the meaning of its name in certain dialects: 'devil'.

Duvel uses the same yeast strain chosen by Victor Moortgat in the 1920s, which actually originates from Scotland. After being cold matured, the beer is bottled, where it undergoes a second fermentation for two weeks in the cellars. Then the beer is moved to cold cellars, where it continues to mature and stabilise for a further six weeks. This particularly long maturation is what gives Duvel its bright, fruity and sharp-tasting flavour profile, which despite its strength, never becomes cloying or tiring.

If carefully poured, leaving the yeast sediment in the bottle, Duvel is a bright and clear golden colour, with its trademark foaming head. The aroma has distinctive banana and toffee notes along with a little spicy kick of clove and orange. It's not a complex aroma, but it is more than enough to whet the appetite.

the facts

Brewer Brouwerij Duvel Moortgat
Origin Antwerp, Belgium
Strength 8.5%
Type Blonde Ale
Web www.duvel.be
Temperature 6-8°C

Duvel has classic Belgian blonde ale flavours of zesty lemon, sticky sweetness, banana, yeasty earthiness and spicy clove, all heightened by the heady alcohol notes that are quite clearly there, and yet do nothing to diminish the speed at which you drink this refreshingly sweet beer. It's not a multi-faceted or very deep beer, but it works as a refreshing, if naughtily strong, bottle at the end of a long day.

Monkfish or sea bass cooked with lemon makes a simple, delicious partner to Duvel, as do Gouda and blue cheeses, where its strength can tackle pungent flavours. Duvel is still a classic Belgian golden ale that's easy to enjoy.

THE BEER TALKING

HEDWIG NEVEN HEAD BREWMASTER AT DUVEL MOORTGAT

What made you want to become a brewer?
I grew up close to Hoegaarden, in the years that Pierre Celis wheat beer became immensely popular. This of course affected me deeply, so I soon started brewing beer for myself, which I continued as a student at the University of Leuven. I was fascinated by the success of Hoegaarden and by Pierre Celis, who was a real genius but remained a very humble and friendly man at the same time…

What do you most enjoy about brewing?
What I like most is that, even while you stick with only the four basic ingredients (water, hops, yeast and malt), the variety and complexity you can give to the beer is almost limitless. So the creativity that you can translate into a final beer is what I enjoy most.

LONDON SOUR DAMSON

An astonishing fruit beer from London's most understated brewery

Whilst there are plenty of beers nowadays with lengthy social media countdowns ("13 more sleeps!") and even lengthier lines to obtain them, some beers come along, unannounced, and just plain blow you away. This is very much the standard operating procedure of London's The Kernel.

Cited as an inspiration by most of the craft brewers in the UK and beyond, Evin O'Riordain's all-but-unbranded brewery is, ironically, one of the most recognisable labels in craft beer. A former cheesemonger, O'Riordain's gifted palate found its true calling when he began to reconstruct vibrantly hoppy American IPAs and historic British dark beers in a railway arch in Bermondsey, London in 2009. Since then The Kernel has established a reputation as a favourite of drinkers and brewers alike, and has experimented in many more styles.

The Kernel's London Sours were originally a handful of different Berliner Weisse-style beers, but The Kernel's mastery of sour beers and mixed fermentation has evolved since then. London Sour Damson is a blend of barrel-aged and freshly brewed saisons, refermented in stainless steel tanks with 350g per litre of damsons and aged for five months.

the facts

Brewer The Kernel Brewery
Origin London, UK
Strength 5%
Type Wild Ale
Web www.thekernelbrewery.com
Temperature 6-8°C

Damsons, for those not familiar, are small, plum-like fruits native to Great Britain, often used in jams and preserves. The beer takes on a lurid, almost neon, magenta colour which seems to glow from within. The damsons' rich, astringent flavour gives the yeasts a lot to work with, and the fruit expresses itself magnificently in this beer, adding sour, tannic, jammy and bright berry notes. The pitch-perfect texture and body is dry enough to let the fruit lead on the palate but has just enough strength to prevent it from becoming overpowering.

This beer's brilliance will hardly come as a surprise to fans of this seminal brewery, but it is a masterclass piece of brewing.

What's the heritage behind Duvel beer?
Duvel was born decades ago, after the First World War. I think we always were true to the authentic recipe, but we invested heavily in process control. Duvel is still brewed like it always was, but the equipment is some of the most modern in Belgium and the surrounding countries.

What's your favourite beer to drink after work?
Honestly, a young and very cold Duvel; my second favourite beer is Orval...

Which beer do you wish you had made?
Orval. I think it is, from a brewer's point of view, a perfect match between flavour, evolution and stability.

Which of your beers would you say best demonstrates who you are as a brewery?
I would say Duvel Tripel Hop; it is a higher version even of Duvel in terms of gravity, hop flavour, bitterness and overall mouthfeel. Again, this one was brewed with only the four basic ingredients.

TARAS BOULBA

It's hard to believe this beer only uses Saaz hops

THE FACTS
Brewer Brasserie de la Senne
Origin Brussels, Belgium
Strength 4.5%
Type Belgian Blonde
Web www.brasseriedelasenne.be
Temperature 6-8°C

Brasserie de la Senne are possibly Brussels' most interesting brewery, making bold and skilfully-brewed beers in classic styles with a twist. Taras Boulba is the brewery's 'Extra Hoppy Ale', a triumphant and delicious showcase for the Saaz hop, which shines in this beer in a way many will never have tasted.

A careful pour – all de la Senne's beers are bottle-conditioned – will reward you with a pale, golden ale with a generous head that should last to the bottom of the glass. Taras Boulba shines like freshly squeezed fruit juice – fitting given its incredibly citrusy aroma. From the Saaz hop alone, Taras Boulba manages to squeeze out lemon, grapefruit, mandarin, lime and orange flavours, each of them clean and juicy. The yeast character running through the beer adds a little banana, pepper and earthiness, but by and large it's a real hop-fest. The light, crisp body zips along nicely, never threatening to interfere with all the fruity flavours. It builds smoothly and sweetly to a crisp, dry, peppery finish that is simply sublime.

THE GOAT
Holy Mountain Brewing, Seattle, USA
Type Saison **Strength** 4.9%

• Holy Mountain's understanding of the time required to make complex farmhouse ales marks them out for greatness. 'Rustic Brett Saison' The Goat is fermented in oak with a mixed culture of yeasts, aged for three months, then refermented in bottle with wild yeast. Hop and grain notes meld with yeasty funk and beguiling, fruity vanilla flavours from the oak.

ACHEL BLONDE 8
Achel Abbey, Kluis, Belgium
Type Belgian Blonde **Strength** 8%

• Achel Abbey became the latest Trappist monastery to take up brewing when they installed a modern brewery in 1998. This reconnected the monks with their brewing heritage which had come to a dead stop during World War I when the Germans seized their equipment to melt down the copper. Achel Blonde 8 is sweet and boozy, with gentle banana, clove and spice aromas, yeast and dried citrus fruits on the taste and a long, lightly bittered finish.

FARMHOUSE IPA
Brouwerij Kees, The Netherlands
Type Farmhouse IPA **Strength** 6%

• The term farmhouse is perhaps thrown about a little overzealously in brewing, with very little beer in this style being produced in actual farmhouses. Regardless it's a great way of describing hybrid styles like this Farmhouse IPA from Brouwerij Kees (pronounced "Kayse"), which combines the berry fruit and funk of Belgian yeast esters with the familiar grapefruit tones of an American-style IPA.

ABBEY ALE
Ommegang, New York, USA
Type Belgian Dubbel **Strength** 8.5%

• The brewery looks Belgian, sounds Belgian, and in blind taste tests the beer has fooled expert beer judges into thinking it is Belgian. Surprisingly, Ommegang is based in Cooperstown, USA. Abbey Ale contains liquorice root, star anise, orange peel, coriander and cumin, making for a darkly delicious and warming ale.

ORO DE CALABAZA
Jolly Pumpkin Artisan Ales, Michigan, USA
Type Sour Golden Ale **Strength** 8%

• Its name means 'Golden Pumpkin', and it's produced by a brewery called Jolly Pumpkin, but Oro de Calabaza is no pumpkin beer. Instead, this "oak aged Michigan sour bière" takes a strong golden ale base and invites it into Chardonnay casks for several months before bottle refermentation. The beer that emerges evokes lemon pith, honey, apples, and white pepper.

SAUVIN BOMB
Liberty Brewing Co., New Zealand
Type New Zealand IPA **Strength** 7%

• Thankfully the contents of a bottle of Liberty Brewing Co's Sauvin Bomb are far more tasteful than its label might suggest, in fact it is one of the most accomplished IPA's being produced in New Zealand. Nelson Sauvin hops shine on and on in this riot of a beer, evoking technicolour flavours of lychee, mango, gooseberry and kiwi fruit that build towards a crescendo of resinous bitterness.

SAISON DUPONT

The template for modern saisons

The success of a particular beer can be difficult to predict. Most brewers hope that one of their range will achieve iconic status, but it rarely happens overnight - except in the case of Saison Dupont in the 1980s. It tapped into a market thirsting for Old World beer styles, especially those with high hop content.

The popularity of Saison Dupont then helped to revitalise the ailing market for farmhouse ales, and new versions inspired by it began to be brewed in both the Old World and the New, with increasingly exotic hop varieties.

Historically, the seasonal farm workers or saisonniers would probably have enjoyed a weaker brew than this 6.5% saison - it's hard to imagine farm workers quaffing something quite this strong all day while scything the fields without the risk of serious injury. However, while the strength and hop content may have increased to suit modem palates, saisons are still wonderfully refreshing beers, delivering crisp fruit flavours as well as spicy, herbal and peppery notes.

While famous for assertive hoppy bitterness, the flavour profile of a saison is defined by its yeast. Dupont's is widely considered to be one of the best farmhouse ale yeasts in the world, and is rumoured to work at a higher temperature than other similar strains.

Many brewers buy the same strain themselves to replicate the uniquely intense, spicy character it imparts. Saison Dupont is a sharp and complex beer: a bright, hazy gold ale using Pilsner malt and Styrian and East Kent Goldings hops. It is best enjoyed in the corked champagne bottle version, which often pops when opening and pours with a lot of fizz, so care is required.

That bountiful head has a sensational farmhouse ale aroma: lemon rind, apple, cloves, and a bready, almost haybam note of freshness. It's an aroma so fresh that it seems to transport you in that very instant to the brewery itself, every single time that your nose reaches the edge of the glass.

The flavour itself is just as profound. It whirls around on the palate, buzzing across the tongue on a tide of zesty citrus and spicy, peppery hops, dispensing delicate peach, grape and apple notes as it goes. Each mouthful is just as crisp and clear as the last. Its energetic and ferociously snappy flavour profile is wonderfully balanced despite its intensity, and the finish to each sip is enormously dry, pithy and spicy.

Farmhouse ales are some of the easiest beers to match food to; the clue is in the word 'farmhouse'. Flavoursome, simple foods, like peppered roast pork and hard cheeses, are saison's best friends. Its intensely crisp carbonation is ideal for cutting through fatty meats, and the sweet, spicy notes of fruit and pepper are exquisite when paired with cheese, especially wine rind-washed varieties.

As a beer, Saison Dupont isn't just the eminent version of its style, but also one that inspired many of the saisons available today. While the regular version is enough to get most beer geeks excited, there is also an occasionally available dry-hopped version of Saison Dupont that ramps the flavour intensity up even higher, adding more fruity ester notes and spicyness.

the facts

Brewer Brasserie Dupont
Origin Hainault, Belgium
Strength 6.5%
Type Saison
Web www.brasserie-dupont.com
Temperature 8-10°C

IV SAISON

Traditional ale with nothing added

Brasserie de Jandrain–Jandrenouille is a new farmhouse brewery based in the Walloon Brabant region of Belgium, south-east of Brussels. It is remarkable among Belgian farmhouse brewers, mainly for its use of imported American hops and its German-style insistence on only four ingredients: water, malt, hops and yeast. Any spiciness or sweetness comes from those four ingredients, and not the addition of cane sugar or spices. The IV Saison is the brewery's original beer, first brewed in 2008, and is a highly-acclaimed new wave saison that packs lots of fruity flavours.

Undergoing a secondary fermentation in a 75cl bottle, IV Saison pours a bright, hazy gold, tinged with amber. Its head is rocky, forming lots of big bubbles that die down to a thin, persistent head of tight foam. The aroma is more like that of a US-hopped IPA or wheat ale: lots of citrus, honey, apricots and peachy notes. The alcohol is barely detectable, and the wilder, barnyard notes are quite spicy and herbal. It has an absolutely stunning nose.

IV Saison is just as wonderfully fresh and fruity on the palate, delivering all the juicy apricot, peach and citrus notes from the nose while retaining the spicy cloves and grassy, peppery hop notes of a classic saison. Despite all this hoppy madness, it retains a lightness and drinkability totally beyond its strength. The beer's finish is not as spicy as more traditional saisons, but still has a grassy, floral, perfumed quality.

Something this zesty, fruity and sweet needs oiliness and fat to cut into. A platter of cured meats, cheeses and fresh bread is the ideal combination to showcase its surprising versatility. In turn it can cut through fattiness, enhance spiciness in meat, lift saltiness from the palate and add a creamy, fruity quality to many soft cheeses. IV Saison is one of those beers that seems destined to define an afternoon of simple pleasures.

the facts

Brewer Brasserie de Jandrain-Jandrenouille
Origin Walloon Brabant, Belgium
Strength 6.5%
Type Saison
Web www.brasseriedejandrainjand-renouille.be
Temperature 8-10°C

THE BEER TALKING

ALEXANDRE DUMONT
HEAD BREWER, BRASSERIE DE JANDRAIN-JANDRENOUILLE

What made you want to become a brewer?
I come from a family of distillers, but after WWII they closed their distillery because soft drinks were taking the market share of beverages. I've always been attracted to fermenting, I like fermentation and the flavours it can develop. I came to the UK to learn English when I was 14, then went back to Belgium with a brewing kit. The next few years were spent poisoning my family with fermenting beverages, from beers to wines and hydromel! Then, when I was 18, I read a book by Michael Jackson and began to elaborate on my beer knowledge; once I had the opportunity, I started a home brewery.

What do you most enjoy about brewing?
I like the underlying background of brewing: it's a wonderful mix of tradition, nature, personality, physical work and patience managed by knowledge and rigour. But what I mostly enjoy is seeing the smiling faces of people when they drink my beer!

What's the inspiration behind IV Saison?
The house is an old farm from the 14th century revamped in the 18th. There has always been a brewery there 'feeding' the workers. The beers brewed in farms during the winter for the summer workers were called 'Saison', because they were seasonal workers. Most types were light in alcohol and held a long time (more than three months) in maturating tanks. The name 'Saison' is a reference to this past. The 'IV' refers to the fact that they're brewed with four basic ingredients (water, barley malt, hops and yeast) so, like the Germans say, it's a 'Reinheitsgebot' beer. There are also four different hops in it. The beer is designed to be a good mix between a modern US beer and a traditional Belgian blond ale.

3 MONTS

Flanders ale matured in wooden barrels

3 Monts is a perfect example of the subtle differences between biere de garde and the closely related saison. Brewed stronger and intended to be stored for longer, 3 Monts is a smooth, sweet, nutty and wonderfully refreshing beer that displays a deft, measured clarity of flavour rarely found in pale beers of this strength.

Although Biere de Garde was likely brewed at Brasserie de Saint Sylvestre for hundreds of years (according to local archives, the brewery predates the French Revolution), the 3 Monts brands was launched in 1985, around the time that saisons and farmhouse ales became popular again in Europe and the US.

The wrapped, corked and caged bottle top is a bit of a puzzle the first time around (carefully push the wire off with both thumbs), but it makes the first taste all the more rewarding. This lively ale pours a bright strawberry blonde, with lots of head, even from a careful pour. As with any bottle-conditioned beer, it is preferable to leave the yeasty sediment behind, but a slight haze to a farmhouse ale is normal. Its aroma is quite strong in alcohol, bready and has a little all-spice to it, along with a distinct hay-like note.

It seems bitter and zesty from the outset, but the sweetness is grainy and cereal-like as much as it is fruity, creating a smooth and moreish palate with a nutty, peppery finish. The alcohol is noticeable but only in the fullness of flavour, rather than an actual alcohol note. This beer actually improves noticeably if left in a dark, cool cupboard for a few extra months. The yeast has more time complete its attenuation, producing cleaner, sharper flavours that make this fairly strong beer even easier to drink.

A Biere de Garde like 3 Monts is perfect for accentuating the sweetness in roasted chicken or pork, and pairs beautifully with a simple chicken casserole, perhaps even with some of the beer in the pot (if you can bear to part with any of it).

the facts

Brewer Brasserie de Saint-Sylvestre
Origin Saint-Sylvestre-Cappel, France
Strength 8.5%
Type Biere de Garde
Web www.brasserie-st-sylvestre.com
Temperature 8-10°C

AECHT SCHLENKERLA RAUCHBIER MARZEN

The definitive starting point for anyone interested in smoked beer

This is where modem smoked beers began! Historically, almost all beers would have been smoked to a degree, as the barley was malted over coal or wood fires; however, as it became easier to kiln malt in smokeless conditions, the desire for smoked beers vanished in favour of cleaner tasting pale ales and pilsner lagers. One exception is the Bamberg region of Germany, where the locals continued to enjoy the local speciality of smoked beers. The curious nature ofBamberg's rauchbiers gradually caught the attention of beer drinkers across the world. The most famous of the Bamberg breweries is Schlenkerla. In the late 1600s it was a tavern where beer was made - a brewpub by today's definitions - and the owners kilned their barley in a smokehouse with the beechwood gathered from the surrounding forests. Six generations on, the Trum family still own and operate the tavern but the brewing has since moved to larger premises. Impressively, the Trums still smoke their own malt. In recent decades, many brewers emulated the rauchbier style, creating their own versions of smoked porters, stouts and lagers to varying degrees of smokiness. Nevertheless, Schlenkerla's classic rauchbier, made in the German lager style with 100% beechwood smoked malt, remains the best for pure, smoky goodness. It's the go-to beer everyone studies when they want to know about the style. That's why they call it 'Aecht', an old German word which means original. Schlenkerla pours with a rich, ruby-chestnut colour that's bright and crisp at the edges and capped with an off-white layer of foam. The aroma is pungent, with beechwood, ash and earthy notes coming to the fore. It sounds overpowering but anyone who enjoys the woody smokiness of applewood smoked cheese will appreciate the rich aroma. The first tasting divides the room, in the same way sour beers do. Rauchbier is a bacon sandwich in a glass; we're talking four, maybe five rashers of smoked bacon, slightly crispy, with a tactical lashing of HP brown sauce between two layers of dark, lightly toasted granary bread. It's either heaven or hell in a glass, depending on your outlook. The intensity of that sensation passes to allow for more refined notes of oak and caramel, ending on a bitter, smoke finish. The body is crisp at cooler temperatures and smoother if warmed up; either serving is good and an example of how personal preference plays a key part. Again, as with sour beers, if you overcome the shock this uncommon beer causes it can soon find a place in your heart. Schlenkerla is also one of the easiest beers to pair with food: its uncompromising smokiness is a perfect partner with smoked cheeses and plates piled high with meat, whether it's German sausages, Italian antipasto or English cold cuts. A mixed plate of Bavarian cheese and cured meats pulled from the fridge and served alongside a chilled Schlenkerla is one of the easiest and finest snacks a man can have on a lazy afternoon.

the facts

Brewer Brauerei Schlenkerla
Origin Bamberg, Germany
Strength 5.1%
Type Smoky Beer
Web www.smokebeer.com
Temperature 6-8°C or room temperature, depending on preference

THE BEER TALKING

MATTHIAS TRUM
BRAUEREI SCHLENKERLA

What's the inspiration and heritage behind Aecht Schlenkerla Rauchbier?
I am lucky in that my ancestors never made the move to modern-style malting. Being able to continue a century-old tradition and upholding this particular recipe, is very rewarding. Furthermore, always having 'one foot in history' is a great compass for gauging everyday work/worries. Just one example: when the current financial crisis started with the collapse of the Lehman Brothers bank, many company owners in Germany became worried, and the general outlook was dim. I myself thought: "Schlenkerla was brewing beer during the Thirty Years' War, the pestilence and witch hunts, and in two World Wars. A failed bank (in the US) is by comparison a negligible event."
What's your favourite beer to drink after work?
For afterwork-thirst? To be honest, water. But after that, beer. And not only Schlenkerla: there are many good craft beers here in Bamberg, Franconia and world wide.

Which of your beers best defines your brewery?
The classic Rauchbier: Aecht Schlenkerla Rauchbier – Märzen.

BETTER OFF RED
Crux Fermentation Project, Oregon, USA
Type Flanders Red Ale **Strength** 7%

• With Better Off Red, Crux Fermentation Project takes on the Flanders Red Ale – a polarising style, thanks to its propensity for vinegar-strength acidity and bite – and adds a Pacific Northwest twist to the style. Namely, Oregon Pinot Noir barrels, where the wild ale ages for 18 months. That time on oak yields a plummy red beer that's tart, but not overwhelmingly so, and bold with dark fruit aromatics.

F4 BRETT FARMHOUSE ALE
Transmitter Brewing, New York, USA
Type Wild Ale **Strength** 6.8%

• With its focus on 'slow beers', Transmitter seem to shrug off the high-velocity, IPA-hype of many of their New York neighbours. Taproom visitors share corked 75cl bottles, dogs snooze by your feet, and there's a relaxed yet confident feel to its beers. F4 uses three different Brettanomyces strains, and, whilst bone-dry, is ripe with shimmering notes of strawberry, melon and pineapple.

CACTOBACILLUS
Wrecking Bar Brewpub, Georgia, USA
Type Gose **Strength** 4.7%

• Wrecking Bar was founded in a historic mansion falling into disrepair, and was renovated into what quickly became Atlanta's favourite brewpub. Its Cactobacillus 'Prickly Pear Gose' is based on Wrecking Bar's Sea Shanty Gose, but conditioned on a huge amount of prickly pear puree. In 'Hotlanta', there are few beers more refreshing than this almost strawberry-sweet and lightly salty sour beer.

SORACHI ACE

The Champagne of beers

Sorachi Ace started as a limited run beer, part of Brooklyn's Brewmaster Reserve series. However, it instantly proved good enough to warrant becoming a permanent edition to the core range, and from the first sip it's easy to see why.

Sorachi Ace comes in an impressive, 750ml (US pint) champagne bottle, complete with metal cage and cork. It really lends itself well to any dinner occasion, jazzing it up with that celebratory feel, and it's truly a drink designed for sharing. Sorachi Ace is a bubbly, lively creature, one that should be enjoyed as fresh as possible. You'll want the whole thing to yourself but the best enjoyment will come from sharing it round and revelling in the freshly-poured zestiness this beer has to offer.

Sorachi Ace is named after the hop used to brew it, a rare hop of Japanese origin that Brooklyn sources from Washington. It has a characteristic lemon flavour that works well in pale ales, wheat beers and saisons. Brooklyn also use a Belgian ale yeast for the initial fermentation and then ferment it again in the bottle with Champagne yeast. It's no wonder it's such a friendly ale.

It pours with a rose gold colour, plenty of carbonation and a good head of creamy froth. The aroma is fresh lemon, lime leaves, grapefruit zest, peach blossom and some pine resin, making for one of the cleanest beer smells going.

From the first mouthful, Sorachi Ace is unlike anything else. The body is crisp at the edges and sweet and sour at the core, with key lime pie notes cutting through on the foretaste, contrasting with an earthy, almost sour tang from the Belgian yeast and a smooth, peachy fruit finish. It crackles with life and energy, which is why this drink is best served fresh and shared around the table as quickly as possible.

the facts

Brewer Brooklyn Brewery
Origin New York, United States
Strength 7.6%
Type Saison
Web www.brooklynbrewery.com
Temperature Serve lightly chilled, 7-9°C

THE BRETT

Little Earth Project, Suffolk, UK
Type Stock Ale **Strength** 10.5%

• By fusing wood ageing, wild yeast and bacteria along with locally grown and foraged ingredients, Little Earth Project is producing some of the most unique beers in the country. 'The Brett' is a stock ale that pays homage to the earthy, tart and curiously complex Brettanomyces yeast strain that uses completely organic ingredients. Ensure you have some incredibly potent cheese nearby when enjoying this beer.

PECHE 'N BRETT

Logsdon Farmhouse Ales, Oregon, USA
Type American Wild Ale **Strength** 10%

• Half a pound of peaches go into every gallon of Logsdon Farmhouse Ales' Peche 'n Brett. The beer begins its life as the Oregon brewery's award-winning Seizoen Bretta before being heavily fruited for your drinking pleasure. Once you manage to crack the wax sealing on the bottle you can expect a ton of pulpy, juicy stone fruit on the palate wrapped up with some barnyard funk and a pleasingly tart acidity.

120 MINUTE IPA

Dogfish Head, Milton, Delaware, USA
Type Barleywine **Strength** 15-20%

• Caution, this way lies hops. Not the juicy, fruity and dank hops you find in today's modern IPAs, but sticky, resinous and tremendously bitter hops that are supported by an immense tower of malt flavour. Its ABV changes annually but you can guarantee there will be plenty of naval orange, candied lemon and a huge grassy bitterness supporting a beer that can support many years of careful ageing.

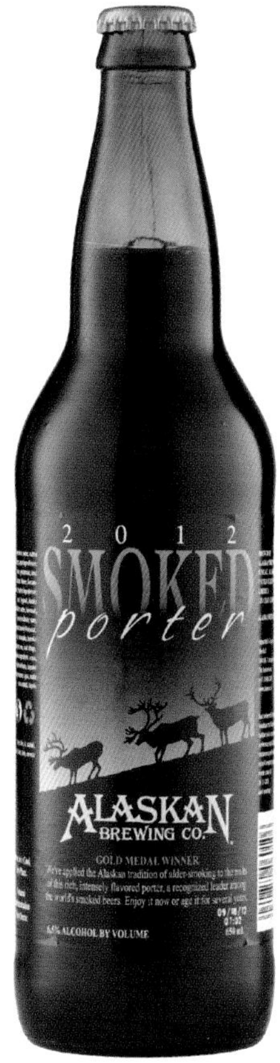

SMOKED PORTER

A very different take on the smoked beer angle

THE FACTS
Brewer Alaskan Brewing Co
Origin Alaska, United States
Strength 6.5%
Type Smoky beer
Web www.alaskanbeer.com
Temperature 12-14°C

Unlike most smoked beers, Alaskan Smoked Porter draws inspiration not from the smoked rauchbiers of the German Bamberg region, but from their own Alaskan heritage. Alaska also enjoyed a gold rush in the 19th century and plenty of breweries were in operation to quench the thirsts of miners and prospectors. None of those early breweries survived the Prohibtion era but their legacy lives on and today the same wood is used to impart complex, smoky qualities on Alaskan Smoked Porter.

It pours with a silky, black body wrapped in a plush head of cappuccino coloured foam. The aroma is reminiscent of peated Islay malt whiskies, with the heathery, medicinal note that comes from peat and accentuated by wood smoke. It's already a different take on the smoked beer angle, set apart from Schlenkerla Rauchbier's woody, meatiness or the chilli heat of Redwillow Smokeless. Fans of peaty Scotch are in for a treat.

Up front it's sweet and velvety on the tongue, a caramelized brown sugar quality reaching the taste buds first. It turns into treacle for a moment before the peated, whisky barrel woodiness cuts through. Peaty, smoked heather flavours are hard to ignore; it's an acquired taste. The smoke quality isn't overpowering, and hardly noticeable at first. It comes about suddenly though, then slowly graduates into dark cherries, toasted granary bread and burnt gingerbread before going out on a mildly dry, bitter liquorice finish.

MAGMA

Why choose between Tripel and IPA?

THE FACTS
Brewer Brouwerij The Musketeers
Origin Ursel, Belgium
Strength 9%
Type Tripel IPA
Web www.themusketeers.be
Temperature 8-10°C

Whilst Belgium produces over 1,600 different beers, many of these fall into fairly traditional styles and recipes from which Belgian brewers will generally not deviate. However, the newer generation of Belgian brewers, like Brouwerij The Musketeers, take their influences from modern craft beer culture, incorporating new ideas, ingredients, styles and techniques as they see fit, and retaining a truly Belgian identity while doing so. Troubadour Magma exemplifies this approach.

The Musketeers brew their beers at De Proefbrouwerij, and are best known for their 'Troubadour' range. Troubadour Magma is a 'Tripel IPA', a rich, dry-hopped amber beer of 9% alcohol that balances the yeast-forward fruitiness of Belgian Tripel with the big hop character of an American IPA. It certainly looks the part of a Belgian Tripel, with its slightly hazy bronze colour and mousse-like foam, but beyond that, it's a very different beast. A heavy-dry-hopping of Simcoe gives Magma its pronounced tropical fruit and resinous pine character, none more so than in its aroma, where it slightly overpowers the honeyed, spice notes of the yeast.

The yeast has a bit more to say in the beer's flavour, where it seems to marshal the competing elements of juicy hop notes, luxuriant grain texture and gentle spiciness into cohesive, singularly vivid fruitiness. There's no booziness exactly, but rather a lingering candied orange note that hints at fruit liqueur.

All of Magma's flavours interlock so neatly that its full-bodied texture becomes almost silky. The combination of hop and yeast notes make it an incredible pairing partner for cheese and charcuterie.

LA FIN DU MONDE

An apocalyptically delicious Belgian style Tripel from one of Canada's finest

THE FACTS
Brewer Unibroue
Origin Chambly, Quebec, Canada
Strength 9%
Type Tripel
Web www.unibroue.com
Temperature 10-12 °C

There were unprecedented bursts of outrage when Japanese brewing giant Sapporo acquired the well-respected Canadian brewery Unibroue in 2006. Some of the Quebec-based brewery's most ardent supporters reacted by emptying the contents of any bottles in their possession into the nearest gutter. However over a decade later many of those who were outraged might be eating their words, as the sublime quality of the beers produced by Unibroue has not decreased one iota. In fact you might go as far as to say that the quality of its beers has only improved.

Unibroue established itself in the Canadian town of Chambly in the province of Quebec in 1993. Since then it has steadily built a strong reputation for producing a range of beers heavily influenced by traditional Belgian brewing methods. This includes Maudite, a strong dark ale and Éphémère, a Belgian-style wit, which is often flavoured with fruit such as apples or raspberries. However, perhaps the crown jewel in Unibroue's range is its Tripel, La Fin Du Monde – which literally translates from French as 'The End of the World'.

You needn't be fearful of this particular beer, however – that is unless you choose to consume it in volumes great enough to give you a hangover that will make you believe the world really is ending. To taste La Fin Du Monde you'll find flavours of white pepper, cloves and red berries, which lead to a rounded, candy sugar sweetness before wiping your palate clean with a dry and lingeringly spicy finish. If you've tried it then it should come as no surprise that this elegant beer has won more medals and awards than any other beer currently produced by a Canadian brewery.

CUVEE DE TOMME

The Lost Abbey Brewing Company, San Marcos, California, USA
Type Strong Ale **Strength** 11%

• It takes a long time for Cuvée de Tomme to arrive in your glass. Made with barley malt, raisins, candi sugar and sour cherries, the beer undergoes a year long secondary fermentation in bourbon barrels, with the addition of more cherries and Brettanomyces. When you indulge in this wine-dark beer, look for beguiling notes of cherry, vanilla, almond, chocolate, and yeasty funk.

NELSON SAUVIN

Mikkeller (at De Proefbrouwerij), Copenhagen, Denmark
Type Bière Brut **Strength** 9%

• Known for eclectic and extraordinary releases, Nelson Sauvignon (sometimes known as Sauvin Brut) is one of Mikkeller's true masterstrokes. Nelson Sauvin hops, known for their grape-like and tannic qualities, shine in this white wine barrel-aged, mixed fermentation beer. Fine, crisp carbonation lifts and sharpens the vinous and tropical fruit notes in this effervescent ale with the character of sparkling wine.

LIQUID MISTRESS

Siren Craft Brewery, Finchampstead UK
Type Red Ale **Strength** 5.8%

• Whilst this dubs itself a Red IPA, Liquid Mistress is really more of a highly-hopped, yet winter-warming red ale, with a beguiling aroma of cherries, chocolate and pine. A thick, luscious malt body, imparting currants, chocolate syrup and red velvet cake makes for a filling mouthful. Then, it blasts your palate with bitterness, spice and more pine, for a powerful and astringently sticky finish that brings you back for more.

RODENBACH VINTAGE

Brouwerij Rodenbach, Roeselare, Belgium
Type Flanders Red Ale **Strength** 7%

• Most of Rodenbach's sour red ales are blends of different proportions of aged and young beer. Vintage, however, is the brewer's selection of a single, two-year-old vat for that year, bottled without blending. Even without the softening contribution of a younger, sweeter beer, Vintage still has some jammy fruitiness, but sharpened by cider vinegar, cranberry, vanilla-like oak and tangy cherry.

AMERICAN BROWN ALE

Runaway Brewery, Manchester, UK
Type Brown Ale **Strength** 5.7%

• The humble brown ale gets far less than its fair share of love from beer fans these days, with pale and hoppy being the style du jour. Step in Manchester's Runaway Brewery with its accomplished American Brown. This satisfyingly caramel hued ale balances notes of pine resin from American hops with a touch of roast and a balanced sweetness leading to a dry finish.

SAISON BERNICE

Sante Adairius Rustic Ales, California, USA
Type Saison **Strength** 6.5%

• "The beer in this bottle is alive," says Saison Bernice's label, and it's true that the brewers at Sante Adairius treat their beers with all the tenderness and care afforded to living beings. As a mixed-fermentation, farmhouse-style beer, Saison Bernice is inoculated with a range of yeasts, including Brettanomyces. As a result, it's rustic and beautifully complex, with notes of hay, tart apple, lemon, and white wine.

DARK RUBY MILD

Sarah Hughes Brewery, Dudley, UK
Type Dark Mild **Strength** 6%

• Besides perhaps the ubiquitous Batham's Bitter, few beers surmise the Black Country as well as Sarah Hughes Dark Ruby Mild. This broodingly crimson ale oozes aromas of malt loaf and fruitcake, which slide onto the palate forming the perfect balance of bitterness and sweetness. This beer is incredibly drinkable on cask, with flavours that belie its 6% ABV.

BLINKER

Siphon Brewing,
Oostkerke, Damme, Belgium
Type Saison **Strength** 5.5%

• Siphon has been brewing for just over a year, with a small yet very polished range of beers to its name. Barley, wheat and local hops form the structure of its simple, elegant Blinker saison, but it's the yeast that does both the heavy lifting and fine-tuning. Delicate citrus notes are kept refreshing by a deliciously crisp texture and bone-dry finish.

SIX DEGREES NORTH TRIPEL

Six Degrees North, Scotland, UK
Type Tripel **Strength** 9%

• Scotland's Six Degree's North draws its brewing inspiration from Belgium, hence the name of their brewery, which lies six degrees north of the country. This Tripel is an indulgent homage to one of Six Degrees North's favourite styles. Weighing in at a hefty 9% alcohol, it's abound with flavours of cotton candy, stone fruit and malt loaf, with plenty of sweetness and white pepper spice in its lingering finish.

SMUTTLABS BRETT & I

Smuttynose Brewing Company,
Hampton, New Hampshire, USA
Type Wild Ale **Strength** 6%

• Smuttynose established Smuttlabs in 2007 as a catchall for its smaller-batch, experimental beers, from barrel-aged numbers to culinary collaborations. Of these limited-edition brews, Brett & I is a recurring highlight. A Belgian strong ale that does time with Brettanomyces in red wine barrels, it's at once funky with the classic Brett farmyard profile while cultivating an almost pineapple-like sweetness.

RESISTANCE

Summer Wine Brewery, Holmfirth,
Yorkshire, UK
Type Dark Mild **Strength** 3.7%

• Yorkshire's, Summer Wine Brewery quickly built a reputation on the back of its American-inspired hop forward ales such as Diablo IPA. However, one of the real treats within its impressive lineup of beers is Resistance, a classic dark mild with a soft and silky body that presents flavours of malt loaf, figs, and a spicy, earthy British hop character.

POPERINGS HOMMEL BIER

Taste the hop fields of Belgium

THE FACTS
Brewer Brouwerij Van Eecke (Leroy Breweries)
Origin Poperinge, Belgium
Strength 7.5%
Type Belgian Strong Golden Ale
Web www.leroybreweries.be
Temperature 6-8°C

One of the reasons Belgian beer is so idolised across the world is the unique, slightly magical sense of place that it evokes. Whilst breweries with cutting-edge equipment and the most recently-developed ingredients can capture attention, many are jealous of the unique connection that Belgian brewers have, to their locality, their methods and ingredients.

Hommelbier ('Hommel' is a local dialect word for hop) was first brewed by brewer Karel Leroy in 1981, to be served at the hop festival that year in the village of Poperinge (and still held there every three years). Using hops only grown in Poperinge (including Brewer's Gold and Challenger), and water drawn from the brewery's own well, it looks every inch the classic Belgian golden ale, with its bright, slightly coppery gold colour and healthy, dense cap of white foam.

The aroma might come as a surprise, though. Alongside the floral yeast character, all kinds of hop notes come leaping out of that foam: hedgerow fruit, white pepper, citrus zest, and something a little like a forest after rainfall. Allow the beer to warm a couple of degrees from fridge temperature and more of that floral yeast and zestiness will come to the fore.

The beer's oily, peppery hop notes glide across the palate on a softly honeyed malt base with accents of orange, and intriguing spice notes at the back of the palate. The high carbonation gives this 7.5% beer a surprising amount of lift, and with its hoppy bite and assertive bitterness, it's all too easy to drink it like a 5% beer. That might just be the magic at work, though. If you can't get enough of Hommelbier's moreish hop character, look out for the 'Dry Hopping' and wet-hopped 'New Harvest' versions of this true beer of origin.

SERPENT

Thornbridge Brewery, Bakewell, UK
Type Wild Ale **Strength** 9.5%

• The incredible Serpent was created by Brooklyn Brewery's Garrett Oliver and Thornbridge Brewery. After brewing a Belgian-style strong golden ale, it was blended with cider lees from Oliver's Cider, and aged in Four Roses bourbon barrels. The result is a totally unique beer with cider or wine-like qualities – poised and finely carbonated, rich with apple, grain and spice.

CURSED

TRVE Brewing Company, Colorado, USA
Type American Sour Ale **Strength** 4.5%

• If you ever find yourself in Denver, do yourself a favour and pop into TRVE Brewing's taproom – it's one of the best bars in the city, especially if you've got a penchant for heavy metal. TRVE brews many different styles, but its mixed fermentation sours, like Cursed, lead the way. Hints of phenolic Belgian yeast dabble with a touch of tangy apricot and lemon juice.

MERRY MONKS

Weyerbacher Brewing Co, Pennsylvania, USA
Type Tripel **Strength** 9.3%

• Founded in eastern Pennsylvania in 1995, Weyerbacher is one of the state's most established craft breweries, and is known for its high-alcohol, Belgian-inflected styles. Merry Monks is its full-throttle take on a classic Belgian tripel. Against a backdrop of biscuity malt, the brewery uses an Abbey yeast strain that yields a complex array of banana, clove, pepper, and apple notes.

TRIPEL VAN DE GARRE

The best House Beer in the world

THE FACTS
Brewer Brouwerij Van Steenberge
Origin Ertvelde, Belgium
Strength 11.5%
Type Belgian Tripel
Web www.degarre.be
Temperature 8-10 °C

So, you're visiting Bruges for the first time, and you've been told to seek out a place called De Garre. You can see where it is on a map, and yet, you keep walking past without finding it. When you eventually find De Garre, down an alley off the street connecting the city's two main squares (Breidelstraat), you'll wonder how you kept walking past without noticing. What manner of sorcery protects this place, and why?

Inside, you'll find one of Belgium's most beautiful beer cafés, with warm autumnal light, rich wooden tones throughout, and best of all, the rolling murmur of pleasant conversation facilitated by glasses of beer. You take a seat, and ask for the house beer, because you were told to do this as well.

The Tripel Van De Garre arrives at your table, in a sturdy, globular glass, looking quite a lot like a white-topped bronze lightbulb. It is sat on a tray (covered with a frilly paper doily, referencing the city's lace trade) alongside a small plate of creamy-tasting cheese. From the dense cloud of foam sat atop the liquid, you smell honey, peppercorns and toffee apple. Sipping through the foam, there's a meringue-like sweetness, sharpened by candied orange, then a little tickle of alcohol, and a dry, oily finish of hops and spice. You eat some cheese, drink some more beer, and repeat.

It's quite likely that you won't realise Tripel Van De Garre is 11.5% until the second glass. Don't worry, this is normal. Take your time. After conversation, more cheese, and more beer, perhaps you'll explore the menu, or perhaps you'll ask for just one more Tripel. Oh, and some more cheese. Perhaps another Tripel.

AMBER ALE

Wiper and True, Bristol, UK
Type Pale Ale **Strength** 5.3%

• Like all of its beers, Wiper and True's elegant series of Amber Ales features a revolving selection of hops and malts. You can usually count on the presence of malted rye, adding both a caramel colour to the beer along with spicy, peppery notes and a touch of sweetness. American hops round out the spice with notes of citrus and tropical fruit, with a peppery finish rounding out their resinous quality.

WHERRY

Woodforde's, Norwich, UK
Type Bitter **Strength** 3.8%

• In peak condition, enjoyed somewhere near its source in East Anglia, Wherry has the feel and taste of home. Its subtle hop notes and malt loaf sweetness come alive when dispensed from a cask given proper care. It simply isn't concerned with being exciting; it only cares about being what it is: a light, uncomplicated English bitter in the traditional style.

PEACEMAKER

Black Project Spontaneous & Wild Ales, Denver, Colorado, USA
Type American IPA **Strength** 7.6%

• For Black Project, creating a beer that reflects the local terroir is of primary importance; to make spontaneously fermented beers, the brewers place wort in coolships, where it can attract passing microflora. Peacemaker is an excellent example of this process. A blend of a wheat beer and a golden ale – both aged in barrels that previously held bourbon and cherry wine – it offers a complex array of fruit, vanilla, and musky yeast notes.

winter

Warmth washes over your face as the door closes behind you. It might be the coldest season, but everything you do in it is about warmth. The beer might be wet and dark, just like the nights, but it doesn't have to be cold. Big, bulbous glasses filled with rich, luxurious stout, decadent, intense porters or perhaps something stronger. It's the time of year that getting comfortable extends to everything you eat and drink.

FLYING DOG
OK LET'S PARTY!
FIRESTONE WALKER
BREWING COMPANY
Est.1996
PROPRIETOR'S VINTAGE
2017
ARABOLA
No. 008
VINTAGE
BARREL-AGED
IMPERIAL
STOUT
12 FL. OZ. (355ML)
DESCHUTES BREWERY
BEND, OREGON
ABYSS
2015 RESERVE

ADAM

A dark and delectable strong ale from one of Portland, Oregon's finest

It's difficult to walk a few yards in Portland, Oregon without finding a great craft beer spot. This eclectic and creatively curious city has become something of a nesting place for craft beer in the United States. At the time this book went to print, there were 84 breweries in the Portland metropolitan area and at the rate at which they're opening that number has probably already increased. In fact, Portland, Oregon has more breweries per capita than any other city in the world and around 60% of the beer sold in the city is classified as 'craft'.

Hair of the Dog was an early adopter in Portland's craft beer culture, setting up shop inside a former fire station, by the banks of the Willamette River in 1993. It built a name for itself on the back of its strong beers inspired by historic styles, many of which take their names from folks in the beer industry that inspired Hair of the Dog's Founder, Alan Sprints.

Perhaps the most well known of Sprints' beers is Adam, the first beer ever produced by Hair of the Dog. Adam is a strong dark ale inspired by a similar, historic style that originated in Dortmund, Germany. It's rich with flavours of molasses, stewed stone fruits and sherry, with a comforting finish that's marked by warming alcohol. It's great on its own or paired with an equally rich and indulgent dessert but according to its creator this beer really comes into its own when paired with a roaring fire and a just lit cigar.

the facts

Brewer Hair of the Dog Brewing
Origin Portland, Oregon, USA
Strength 10%
Type Strong Dark Ale
Web www.hairofthedog.com
Temperature 14-16°C

GONZO IMPERIAL PORTER

A bruiser of an American porter that's certainly not to be trifled with!

Flying Dog Ales has produced some of the best bottle labels in the world of craft beer. It hired Ralph Steadman to do its artwork, the British cartoonist best known for his work with the *Fear & Loathing in Las Vegas* author Hunter S Thompson, and the words of the late anarcho-journalist are the firm's mantra: "Good people drink good beer."

The label on the Gonzo Imperial Porter bottle features a guy with a skull for a face, an homage to Thompson himself, who drank straight Wild Turkey and purportedly chewed human adrenal glands as a morning pick-me-up. From the outset, then, this is being established as a big, powerful brew.

Gonzo is black with a heavy gravity that pulls in the light and makes it that little bit darker. The body is oil thick and oozes into the glass, topped by a tarry, mocha-coloured head that levels out into a smooth, creamy consistency.

The aroma is big, juicy American hops and malts, with umami notes of soy sauce and thick, sweet smells of molasses, treacle and candy being the dominant force. There's also an oily hop aroma, with bags of strong, sweet liquorice, a hint of almond and a warming, boozy hit.

The body is dense and alcoholic, sticking to the lips and rewarding the drinker with unexpected bursts of flavour. Initially Gonzo delivers brown sugar, cream, coffee, chocolate and almonds, which all add up to a decadent, Irish coffee liqueur experience. Over time, it takes a dark turn, becoming resinously hoppy with booziness in the finish.

This is a fine beverage, and one the good Dr Thompson would be proud of. It's a bold example of an American porter – a heavyweight battlecruiser of a beer, full of enough punch and flavour to take your face off and leave a grinning skull.

the facts

Brewer Flying Dog Ales
Origin Maryland, USA
Strength 9.2%
Type Porter
Web www.flyingdogales.com
Temperature 12-16°C

HUNAHPU'S IMPERIAL STOUT

A viscous, bold, and heavily spiced stunner of an imperial stout

Hunahpu's Imperial Stout is one of the best-rated and most desired examples of the style in the United States, if not the world. The reason for the fervour is two-fold. First is the beer's rarity: released just once a year at the official Hunahpu's Day event – for which tickets begin at $200, and are capped at 4,000 attendees – the beer isn't otherwise sold online, at the tasting room, or distributed beyond the brewery. If you don't manage to get ahold of tickets to Hunahpu's Day yourself, then, your options are restricted to bottle shares or trades. First released in 2010 to a group of just 250 drinkers, Hunahpu's is, after seven short years, nothing short of a phenomenon.

But extraordinary hype is only one part of the equation. The second reason for Hunahpu's incredible success is, simply, that it's a world-class imperial stout.

Brewer Wayne Wambles tinkered with the recipe for several years prior to its official release; thick and sticky as tar, and just as black in the glass, it's the kind of brew that overwhelms the palate with its velvet potency. Named in honour of the Mayan god Hunahpu, it's also imbued with a delectable array of spices and other flavourings, including cacao nibs, Madagascar vanilla beans, cinnamon, ancho chillies, and pasilla chillies (ingredients that the Mayans – the first to produce and consume chocolate – would certainly recognise). To pour a snifter of this beer is akin to sitting down to a very thick, very decadent molten chocolate lava cake. Chocolate is the first thing to hit the palate, followed by a ripple of deep espresso roastiness. Cinnamon spice and fragrant vanilla are beautifully integrated, while the chilli heat only makes itself known at the conclusion of the sip, leaving a warm simmer at the back of the throat.

the facts

Brewer Cigar City Brewing
Origin Tampa, Florida, USA
Strength 10.2%
Type Imperial Stout
Web www.cigarcitybrewing.com
Temperature 10-12°C

CIGAR CITY BREWING®

RASPUTIN

A world-class Russian imperial stout that's sweet, chocolaty, and utterly decadent

A Russian imperial stout by any other name would taste as sweet as Brouwerij De Molen's Rasputin – which is a good thing, considering just how many monikers this beer has adopted over the years.

De Molen brews beautiful stouts, and Rasputin may represent one of its finest achievements to date. But the beer isn't without its controversy. Though it began life as Rasputin, in a nod to the style's historic associations with Russia, a cease-and-desist letter from California's North Coast Brewing – who make an Old Rasputin imperial stout – inspired a rebrand. The stout was briefly, cheekily redubbed 'Disputin' before it became the straightforward 'Cease and Desist'. These days, you're likely to find it on the shelves as 'Moord & Doodslag', which sounds like it should translate to a dirty joke but, in fact, means 'Murder & Manslaughter' in Dutch. Cheery stuff.

Confusion over identity aside, this beer is more than deserving of a place in your cellar. Its name suggests a brutal sort of intensity, but this Russian imperial stout is redolent of chocolate and unabashed in its sweetness. Infused with toasty coffee notes, it also offers a plummy array of jammy, dark fruit flavours. You may also detect raisins, a hint of vanilla, and a subtly tobacco-rich smokiness on the palate. Serve it in place of dessert at your next dinner party, though be sure to share: despite clocking in at over 10% ABV, this beer integrates its alcohol beautifully, and it's easy to forget its potency.

It's possible that the beer's name will have undergone a few new evolutions by the time the brewery recommends removing it from your cellar; on the label, De Molen writes that it can be aged for up to 25 years. Expect it to develop in maturity and complexity with every passing year, moving from up-front sweetness to an abiding, sherry depth.

the facts

Brewer Brouwerij De Molen
Origin Bodegraven, The Netherlands
Strength 10.4%
Type Imperial Stout
Web www.brouwerijdemolen.nl/
Temperature 10-12°C

FULLER'S VINTAGE ALE (2010)

The most respected and collected vintage ale in Britain

London is teeming with a population explosion of new breweries, but the Daddy Cool of the bunch is Fuller's. The company is based at the Griffin Brewery, in Chiswick, London. The brewery has stood there for a long time and is believed to be over 350 years old.

Commonly known as Fuller's, the brewery has been making a vintage ale since 1997. It's the same but different each year, with the hops and malt subtly shifting in quantity and variety. Fuller's choose the finest ingredients that year has to offer and occasionally chase up a contemporary theme. Each new batch is Fuller's to the core but unique enough to capture renewed interest.

This review is based on a bottle of the 2010 vintage. Brewed with Fuggles, Styrian Golding and Target hops, it presents a polished, oaky colour with a dense head of foam that leaves behind plenty of lacing on the glass. Providing you don't rouse the yeast from its slumber, it's a surprisingly clear and well conditioned beer, with a head that audibly crackles at the outset. The aroma is delightful, and nowhere near as intense as some strong ales can be. It gives out deep notes of Christmas cake, nuts, chocolate, and a red wine or sherry aroma, with some yeastiness, dark granary bread and biscuits far in the background.

Marmalade on toast, apples, pears and crystallised fruits come through in the foretaste. That's followed by a big, malt body lifted up by a warming boozy oomph in the midsection, which rides off into the long, lingering sherry aftertaste.

The midsection is where the real action is. The cured fruits and sherry notes are impressive, but this vintage is a guided tour of what malt can offer. From crackers to toffee to fresh bread, it's all here. No wonder people buy crates of each release.

the facts

Brewer Fuller's
Origin London, UK
Strength 8.5%
Type Vintage Ale
Web www.fullers.co.uk
Temperature 12-16°C

THE ABYSS

Open this beer and embrace the darkness but pray it does not take your soul

When does a beer cease to become more than simply a beer? Perhaps when the final product is something that is greater than the sum of its parts. In brewing, blending is a true art form that is attempted by some but only truly mastered by a select few. Brewers can study best brewing techniques and practices as well as learn fermentation science inside and out – but when it comes to blending there is only one thing to trust – your palate.

One wonderful example of the fine art of blending beer is The Abyss, an imperial stout from Bend, Oregon's Deschutes – a brewery perhaps better known for its core beers such as Fresh Squeezed IPA and Black Butte Porter. The Abyss is a seasonal beer that the brewery releases annually and is almost certainly a beverage that can be described as greater than the sum of its parts. It's a complex beer even before it spends time in barrels, featuring six types of malt, four hop varieties plus the addition of black strap molasses, brewer's liquorice, vanilla beans and cherry bark.

Fifty per cent of the final blend then spends the better part of the next 12 months in Bourbon, Pinot Noir and virgin Oregon oak barrels. It's then masterfully blended back to form the finished product. As you'd expect, The Abyss pours oubliette black, releasing the aromas from the additions of molasses, liquorice and vanilla as it oozes from the bottleneck. These flavours mingle on the palate along with warming alcohol before leading to a tannic, bourbon and red wine tinged finish. It's an incredibly complex beer, but given time to warm and open up the flavours will soften and you too will finally be able conquer and enjoy The Abyss.

the facts

Brewer Deschutes Brewery
Origin Bend, Oregon, USA
Strength 11.1%
Type Imperial Stout
Web www.deschutesbrewery.com
Temperature 14-16°C

PARABOLA

A dark and intense homage to the bourbon barrel

In many cases it's a brewer's job to show restraint – to balance a distinctive set of flavours and wrap them up in a clean and drinkable package. Sometimes, though, a brewer will exercise his or her license to push the intensity of a beer's flavour as far as it can possibly go. Firestone Walker's annually released bourbon barrel-aged stout, Parabola, is just such a beer.

Brothers in law Adam Firestone and David Walker founded Firestone Walker in the town of Paso Robles, California in 1996. Walker, a Brit, brought with him a love for traditional British ales when he moved to California, which was then fused with the American sensibilities of Firestone, whose family were and still are in the wine-making business. It was perhaps the influence of wine-making that inspired this brewery to begin Firestone Walker Barrelworks, one of the most accomplished barrel-ageing projects in beer.

Parabola is already a formidable beer before it spends the better part of a year maturing within oak casks that were formerly used in the production of bourbon. The beer is added to still 'wet' casks, meaning that there's a small amount of bourbon known as the 'devil's cut' still present in the wood. As the barrel expands and contracts with temperature, beer is taken into the wood and mingles with the flavours of bourbon and vanilla from the oak itself. These flavours are rounded out by molasses-sweet notes from the malt, with a finish that provides the lingering taste of fresh pipe tobacco. At 14.5%, Parabola is a beer to be sipped and savoured, just like a fine wine.

the facts

Brewer Firestone Walker
Origin Paso Robles, California, USA
Strength 14.5%
Type Imperial Stout
Web www.firestonebeer.com/
Temperature 14-16°C

MEANTIME LONDON PORTER

English bitter fused perfectly with American Pale Ale

Something that sets Meantime apart is that they make an extra effort to make you feel special. When you get your hands on one of their beers in a shop, it's very hard to put it down. Their beautiful, champagne-corked, oversized bottles add a sense of grandeur to the occasion of simply 'opening a beer'. London Porter is no different in that regard.

The liquid itself is majestic. A classic-porter-black, but tinged with crimson. Naturally, the pillowy clouds of head are tan in colour. The beer only needs to be within a good foot of your nose for its aromas to take hold: thick, wild, almost-sour notes and floral hops fused with bitter berries, dark chocolate and a coffee punch. If you're thinking, 'like most other porters, then?' you would be right. But what separates porters is not just the flavour, but their attitude. A truly great porter is measured by its methods.

Meantime's London Porter is a nimble prize fighter that annihilates its opponents with skill, and most importantly, raw power. From the first bell, this porter is on your gums, throwing belting blows of chocolate, coffee, chocolate, coffee, and hooks of vanilla, spice, blackcurrants and brown sugar. How does it switch back and forth? Relentlessly. Pungent bittering hops follow this onslaught, ending with a finish that somehow is even greater than the sum of its parts.

But there's more. After the finish is an aftertaste of bitter, darkest chocolate, which sits on your tongue for several minutes. It's perfect for pairing with oysters, sticky barbecue ribs and the strongest-tasting meat you can find.

This is a furious and complex beer, retaining authenticity without compromising its ferocity and flavour.

the facts

Brewer Meantime Brewing Co
Origin London UK
Strength 6.5%
Type Porter
Web www.meantimebrewing.com
Temperature 12-16°C

ANCHOR PORTER

The British may have invented porter but Anchor Porter brought it back in style

In the UK, the efforts of CAMRA and Michael Jackson encouraged British breweries to take up the forgotten porter style of beer, with Penrhos Brewery and Timothy Taylor both launching porters in 1978 and Sam Smith's releasing Taddy Porter in 1979. By the late 1980s, more than 60 brewers had a porter in production. It was a proud return to a noble tradition for British brewers. But not content with beating the Russians to the Moon, the Americans also beat the British in the great Porter race. In 1972, Anchor Brewery first trialled their Porter, and by 1974 it was available to buy.

Anchor Porter pours an obsidian black beer. The aroma is luxurious and full of Christmas cake goodness, with raisins, currants, figs and plums sweetened by molasses, treacle and brown sugar.

The mouthfeel is viscous, velvety and soothing. Backing up this claim is a rich taste of molasses and treacle, followed by currants, raisins and plums, while a touch of booze lurks in the background. These qualities all combine to create a dense, fruit malt loaf or Christmas pudding flavour. In the final moments, a flame is set to this brandied cake bomb and warm, toasted malt takes over the tongue. The finish is bittersweet, leaning toward a brown sugar note. This is one of the finest porters out there by far.

the facts

Brewer Anchor Brewing Co
Origin San Francisco, California, USA
Strength 5.6%
Type Porter
Web www.anchorbrewing.com
Temperature 12-16°C

BLACK METAL

The delicious dark side of American farmhouse brewing

Texas' Jester King, which is dedicated to authentic farmhouse ales and, more recently, spontaneous fermentation, has its sights set firmly on the future. Not content with just brewing farmhouse-style ales, Jester King have purchased 58 acres of farmland surrounding the brewery. The plan is to not only grow crops for use in brewing, but to eventually open a winery, distillery and farm-to-table restaurant. Along the way, they've brewed a wide range of esoteric beers with a focus on agriculture, locality and innovation.

Black Metal is a 'Farmhouse Imperial Stout', and whilst brewing stouts using wild yeasts isn't entirely new (in fact, early Russian Imperial Stouts would certainly have had some wild yeast character), Jester King's is unique. Previous versions of the beer used English ale yeast and French saison yeast, but it now uses the brewery's house mixed culture of microorganisms. This culture includes yeast and bacteria harvested from the air and wildflowers from the land around the brewery.

The oil-black liquid has the slightest mahogany tinge, and a lively head of foam. The heady aroma of forest fruits, ground coffee and cocoa powder is tinged with earthy barnyard notes, and its rich body of figs, roast and liqueur chocolates has a prickly, crispy texture. There's also some tart fruitiness and notes of dates that come through as the beer warms up. The mixed culture makes its presence known, but in a supportive way that adds character without clipping the wings of this big stout.

But is it really 'black metal'? Well, the crispy mouthfeel might be the fast-picking guitarist, the rich palate could be the machine-gun bass, and that slight booziness may function as a blast-beat drummer. Thankfully, since there's no rough finish or astringency, the hoarse-voiced vocalist must have phoned in sick.

the facts

Brewer Jester King Brewery
Origin Austin, Texas, USA
Strength 9.1%
Type Imperial Stout
Web www.jesterkingbrewery.com
Temperature 10-12°C

SPEEDWAY STOUT

Sensory nourishment is not in short supply

San Diego's Alesmith don't do small beers. This brewery, founded in 1995, has a reputation for brewing huge beers with colossal flavours. Every brew seems to tower over its neighbours on the shelf. It's not just the bottles that are large, either. Most of their beers are over 8.5%, and Speedway Stout is one of the biggest of the lot. It's a multiple-award-winning crowd pleaser that, through some form of insane magic, combines the intense flavour profile of an imperial stout with the rich, moreish and almost smooth quality of a dry stout.

It's about as black as a beer can be, with a mocha-coloured head that's extremely lively when poured. Speedway's aroma is a heady, boozy one. Between the coffee and liquorice notes, there are tantalising scents of blackberries and brandy. Chocolate is there, but as a deep, roasted, bitter note buried beneath.

A single sip is all you need to feel like blackberries, spices, dark chocolate and espresso are jumping up and down on your taste buds. There's no subtlety to its flavour, and there shouldn't be. Yet there's a warming quality that makes it slightly easier-to-drink than you might expect. The dry, hoppy and roasted notes in the finish give it a much lighter, quenching quality.

If you can keep up with its somewhat crazy attitude, you'll find a firm and loyal friend in Alesmith's Speedway Stout.

the facts

Brewer Alesmith Brewing Co
Origin San Diego, California, USA
Strength 12%
Type Imperial Coffee Stout
Web www.alesmith.com
Temperature 12-16°C

MILK STOUT NITRO

A sweet and luxurious beer that deserves its title of 'America's Stout'

Colorado is one of the most brewery-diverse states in the US. Great beer, along with great bars and taprooms in which to find it, is part of everyday life within the Mountain State. It should come as no surprise then that Colorado is home to some of the largest and most successful breweries in North America, such as New Belgium, Odell Brewing and Oskar Blues.

One of the most well-known Colorado breweries is Left Hand Brewing. Business partners Eric Wallace and Dick Doore founded Left Hand in the town of Longmont, Colorado in 1990 and as of 2017 it's the country's 44th largest craft brewer by sales volume according to the Brewers Association of America.

While Colorado's other craft brewing greats were busy brewing citrus-forward and lip-smackingly bitter IPA, Left Hand did so on the back of a dark and delicious stout. That point of difference has always been what has made this brewery stand out from the crowd and to date Milk Stout accounts for 50% of its production.

In 2011, Left Hand released a bottled version of its Milk Stout that utilised nitrogen, instead of carbon dioxide to gas the beer – just like in popular mass-produced stouts such as Guinness. Nitrogen bubbles are smaller than carbon dioxide bubbles and so add a luxuriously smooth and creamy mouthfeel to this beer, complementing the notes of sweet milk chocolate and bitter coffee. Don't forget to 'pour hard' as the brewery puts it, when emptying a bottle into a glass in order to wake up the nitrogen and properly savour this delectably smooth beer.

the facts

Brewer Left Hand Brewing Company
Origin Longmont, Colorado, USA
Strength 6%
Type Milk Stout
Web www.lefthandbrewing.com
Temperature 8-10°C

EXPEDITION STOUT

Bell's Brewery, Kalamazoo, Missouri, USA
Type Russian Imperial Stout **Strength** 10.5%

• Bell's Expedition Stout is a good candidate for ageing; after a couple of years in the cellar, its rich, roasty bitterness softens into sonorous chocolate, a bouquet of dark fruits, and deep notes of coffee. But even when freshly bottled, this rich and flavourful stout offers a beguiling complexity, as well as a more distinct hop presence than many other examples of the style.

BUSH DE NUITS

Brasserie Dubuisson, Pipaix, Belgium
Type Belgian Strong Ale **Strength** 13%

• There's little fuss surrounding the barrel-ageing programme that exists beneath the Brasserie Dubuisson restaurant – however those that know all agree it produces some of the finest barrel-aged beer in the world. Bush de Nuits (or Scaldis de Nuits in the US) matures for six to nine months in Burgundy barrels, which lend notes of vinous fruit and tannin to this indulgently dark Belgian beer.

COFFEE & CIGARETTES

Cellarmaker Brewing Company,
San Francisco, California, USA
Type Smoked Coffee Porter **Strength** 7.7%

• Cellarmaker describes Coffee & Cigarettes as "a breakfast and dessert beer," and – just like its namesake – it's tempting to enjoy it both upon waking and before bed. Coffee has rarely had a better starring role than in this lightly smoked porter, where it imparts roastiness, rich chocolate, and enough acidity to help counterbalance the beer's decadent creaminess.

MILK STOUT

The Duck-Rabbit Craft Brewery,
Farmville, North Carolina, USA
Type Milk Stout **Strength** 5.7%

• The Duck-Rabbit specialises in dark beers, and its best-selling brew is this traditional take on lactose-dosed stout. Thanks to those residual milk sugars, this pitch-black beer has the kind of creamy, subtle sweetness that'll make you want to lick your lips after every sip. Reminiscent of nostalgic treats like chocolate milk, it's got just enough roasty bitterness to remind you that it's come of age.

ISSEKI NICHO PINOT NOIR

Brasserie Dieu du Ciel, Montreal, Canada
Type Imperial Black Saison **Strength** 9.5%

• Describing Montreal's Brasserie Dieu du Ciel's Isseki Nicho as complex would be doing this multifaceted beer a disservice. Perhaps its finest iteration is the pinot noir barrel-aged version, which combines flavours of red wine, oak, dark chocolate, roasted coffee with hints of funky Belgian yeast before leading to a bone dry finish. Deceptively drinkable for its lofty 9.5% ABV.

10 QUADRUPEL

Fort Lapin, Bruges, Belgium
Type Belgian Quadrupel **Strength** 10%

• One of the lesser-known modern Belgian brewers, Fort Lapin fuses the country's strong brewing tradition with a modern twist. Its 10 quadrupel is a great example of this, using clove, vanilla, coriander seed, cinnamon and juniper to spice this beer. On tasting the beer you'll detect hints of vanilla and molasses, a snap of herbal juniper berry and plenty of roasted coffee and chocolate from the dark malts.

HEL & VERDOEMENIS

Brouwerij de Molen, Bodegraven,
The Netherlands
Type Imperial Stout **Strength** 10%

• The name of Brouwerij de Molen's flagship imperial stout may translate to 'Hell and Damnation' in English, but that's not an accurate description of what it's like to pour out an inky glass of this beer, swirl to admire its sticky viscosity, and bring it to your lips. Vanilla, smoke, sherry, chocolate, brown sugar: it's an utterly decadent tour de force.

TWO HUNDRED FATHOMS

Galway Bay Brewery, Galway, Ireland
Type Imperial Stout **Strength** 10%

• Two Hundred Fathoms is a collaboration between Ireland's Galway Bay Brewery and the Teeling distillery that was launched in 2015 to critical acclaim. This deep, dark stout possesses qualities of molasses, dark chocolate and leather, which are joined by notes of oak, vanilla and honey-sweetness thanks to its time maturing in Teeling Whiskey barrels. Catch it if you can, as this annual release is produced in small batches that sell out quickly.

OLD RUFFIAN BARLEY WINE

Great Divide Brewing Company, Denver, Colorado, USA
Type American Barleywine **Strength** 10.2%

• Great Divide's Old Ruffian Barley Wine is about as subtle as a brass marching band at 3 o'clock in the morning, but for all its bombast, this barleywine is exceptionally delicious stuff. Mahogany-hued and heavy on the caramel and port flavours that this style would typically call for, it's also delightfully hoppy, with a lingering bitterness that remains long after the final sip.

YETI

Great Divide Brewing Co., Denver, Colorado, USA
Type Imperial Stout **Strength** 9.5%

• It turns out you don't need to venture into the forests of the Rocky Mountains to find the elusive Yeti – because it's on tap in Denver, Colorado. This imperial stout from Great Divide uses masses of hops to build a towering, pine-like bitterness around a framework of leather, pipe tobacco, molasses and liquorice. Yeti's dry finish makes it superb with red meats and blue cheeses.

ARBOR BREAKFAST STOUT

Arbor Ales, Bristol, UK
Type Oatmeal Stout **Strength** 7.4%

• Arbor Breakfast Stout. Strong, alluring coffee aromas rouse the nostrils, while a big, boozy, bitter coffee thump shakes the palate awake. It then simmers down to warm milk chocolate, edged by roast malt and a bitter herb finish. Perfect for recovering from the night before and getting back in the game.

B.O.R.I.S. THE CRUSHER

Hoppin' Frog, Akron, Ohio, USA
Type Imperial Stout **Strength** 9.4%

• There are times when all you want is a pint of something crisp and refreshing, there are others when it's time to pour a glug of something indulgent into a large snifter. When that time comes around, help yourself to a glass of B.O.R.I.S. (Brown Oatmeal Russian Imperial Stout) the Crusher from Ohio's Hoppin' Frog. Its intense flavours of dark chocolate, fresh pipe tobacco and molasses are ideally paired with a roaring fire on a dark, cosy evening.

BUXTON IMPERIAL BLACK IPA

Buxton, Derbyshire, UK
Type Pale Ale **Strength** 7.5%

• A black India Pale Ale? No, it's best not to think about it. Just pour it into a glass and marvel at the hoppy, tropical fruit aromas emanating from this midnight hued ale, riding alongside a gentle coffee, treacle and roasted malt bitterness. The taste successfully juggles big American hop flavours of pine, grapefruit and passion fruit with porter-like roast malt and chocolate. It ends on a lingering, citrus and pine bitter finish.

EDMUND FITZGERALD

Great Lakes Brewing Co, Ohio, USA
Type Porter **Strength** 6%

• This popular porter takes its name from a carrier ship that sunk in the waters of Lake Superior during a storm in 1975; where flavour is concerned, you can certainly expect depth and profundity, then. Dark in hue – with a java-coloured head – but of medium body, this drinkable porter provides all the notes of coffee, chocolate, and dark fruits you'd seek from the style.

DARK HORIZON

Nøgne Ø, Norway
Type Dark Ale **Strength** 15-18%

• People know you mean business when you bring this out, and at this strength you had better be sharing. Dark Horizon is a limited edition release, each version a different take on the last. Made using a ton of brown sugar, coffee beans and wine yeast, it tends to be a velvety, dessert-wine style liquid, with luxuriant coffee, chocolate, raisin and liquorice flavours. Lavish.

WORLD WIDE STOUT

Dogfish Head, Delaware USA
Type Stout **Strength** 15-20%

• Before BrewDog grabbed headlines with Tactical Nuclear Penguin, Dogfish Head had reached the scene some ten years earlier with World Wide Stout. The difference is that World Wide Stout remains in production not as a novelty gimmick but as a respected beer. Deep black in colour, it has brandied Christmas fruits, sarsaparilla and hints of booze in the aroma, with a chewy body of malt, figs, raisins, liquorice and plenty of throat-warming alcohol.

BIG ASS MONEY STOUT

Lervig Aktiebryggeri, Stavanger, Norway
Type Imperial Stout **Strength** 17.5%

• Partners in crime Lervig and Evil Twin got into hot water over adding frozen pizza and paper currency to this monstrous super-stout, but the result somehow stands head and shoulders above the shenanigans in its creation. Sumptuously rich in body, drinking this beer is like eating chocolate donuts, lava cake and brandy-soaked Christmas pudding all at once. A mischievous exercise in decadence.

PARADOX

BrewDog, Aberdeenshire UK
Type Stout **Strength** 15%

• Paradox is a barrel-aged imperial stout that uses different whisky distillery's used barrels with each bottling. The current expression using Isle of Arran whisky casks imparts rich honey, molasses, vanilla and toffee notes to an already lavishly luscious stout like mocha with two shots of espresso. Past bottlings have used Smokehead and Jura casks, and quickly become collector's items. These decadent stouts are perfect for further ageing at home.

FOUNDERS BREAKFAST STOUT

Founders Brewery, Michigan, USA
Type Stout **Strength** 8.3%

• What is it with breakfast stout being stupendously strong? Arbor Ale's Breakfast Stout weights in at 7.4% ABV, and Founders' Breakfast Stout tops that. Starting the day on this is also likely to be the end of it, but a good end all the same. Breakfast Stout is full of coffee beans, with an inviting aroma and smooth, though very bitter, taste of coffee, chocolate and a hint of booze.

OLD RASPUTIN

North Coast Brewing Co., Fort Bragg, California, USA
Type Russian Imperial Stout **Strength** 9%

• The legend goes that Russian imperial stouts – huge, burly beers of intimidating strength, richness, and bitterness – were first brewed in England during the 18th century for export to Russia and the Baltics. North Coast infuses its Old Rasputin with this lore, while crafting an exceptional, treacle-black brew that warms as it assails the palate with bitter espresso and dark chocolate.

FULLER'S LONDON PORTER

Fuller's, London, UK
Type Porter **Strength** 5.4%

• First brewed in the 1990s by London's longest surviving brewery, London Porter is light in body to deliver the refreshing quality that early porters were famed for, while carrying with it a heavy load of toffee, brown sugar balanced by a gentle bitterness, burnt wood and roasted malt. There's also a cracking Porter Beef Stew recipe on the Fuller's website that is perfect for a wintry Sunday.

DARK ISLAND RESERVE

Orkney Brewery, Quoyloo, Orkney Islands, UK
Type Strong Scotch Ale **Strength** 10%

• Settings for breweries don't get much more dramatic than the Neolithic sites of the Orkney Islands. Almost as epic as the place itself, Dark Island Reserve is Orkney's rich, high-strength Scotch ale. Three months ageing in Dalmore whisky barrels gives the beer a heady nose of smoke, spice and leather, while fruitcake, treacle and chocolate flavours smother the palate.

GREASE MONKEY

Panhead Custom Ales, Wellington, New Zealand
Type Old Ale **Strength** 8.4%

• Given that Panhead was launched out of a former Dunlop tyre factory, it's appropriate that a mechanical vocabulary pervades its brews. Like the rich and viscous Grease Monkey, which pours the colour of oil but is, happily, much more fun to drink. Raisin, treacle, tobacco, and leather are only some of the flavour notes that can be detected in this unctuous, oak-barrel-aged old ale.

ABRAXAS

Perennial Artisan Ales, St. Louis, Missouri, USA
Type Imperial Stout **Strength** 10%

• Perennial Artisan Ales add ancho chilli peppers, cacao nibs, vanilla beans and cinnamon sticks to its annually released Abraxas imperial stout, ensuring this deliciously dark and indulgent beer will keep the winter chill away from your door. Hints of bitter chocolate, cinnamon and vanilla mingle with notes of molasses and pipe tobacco, with the chilli adding a satisfying trickle of heat.

MOCHACCINO STOUT

Pilot, Leith, Scotland

Type Stout **Strength** 5.5%

• Scotland's Pilot are perhaps better known for their often amusing Twitter antics than they are for making beer – but they're very good at both. Mochaccino Stout fuses hops and grain with coffee, cacao nibs and vanilla imbuing this satisfying rich stout with sweet flavours of chocolate and vanilla ice cream, leaving a satisfying tingle of bitter roasted coffee on your palate in its finish.

OO

Põhjala, Tallinn, Estonia

Type Baltic Imperial Porter **Strength** 10.5%

• Öö is Estonian for 'night', a fitting name for this midnight-black imperial porter from the Baltics. Põhjala use six different grains and Demerara sugar to build the formidable body of this powerful beer, giving it a surprisingly fruity nose amongst caramel and smoke. The flavours are massive but well-defined, dealing out heavy blows of burnt toffee, dark chocolate and stewed fruit.

OLD FREDDY WALKER

Moor Beer Company, Somerset UK

Type Old Ale **Strength** 7.3%

• Old Freddy Walker launched the micro-brewery to fame when it won Winter Beer of the Year in 2004. The recipe has since been tweaked and the awards have continued to pile in. Old Freddy Walker is a dark beer, tinged with a blackcurrant glow, and gives plenty of Christmas pudding, liquorice and treacle on the nose. The taste is an expertly balanced blend of coffee, winter fruits, smoky whispers and a smooth, dry finish.

SAINT PETERSBURG

Thornbridge, Derbyshire UK

Type Imperial Russian Stout **Strength** 7.7%

• The name Saint Petersburg is doubly appropriate – strong English stouts were once shipped to the Czar's court in St. Petersburg over the icy Baltic seas, and a former owner of Thornbridge's stately home headquarters once traded goods with the same city. Saint Petersburg is a complex beast, full of wood, fire and peat, along with the traditional burnt offerings of coffee, malt, chocolate and liquorice leading to a long, bitter finish.

BOMB!

Prairie Artisan Ales, Krebs, Oklahoma, USA

Type Imperial Stout **Strength** 13%

• At 13%, this imperial stout is about as shy and retiring as its exclamatory name would indicate. Aged on coffee, cacao nibs, vanilla beans, and ancho chilli peppers, Bomb! is a warming caress of a beer, piqued with a devilish flicker of heat. Though it has the same colour and viscosity as soya sauce, this stout is pure dessert on the nose and the palate.

CARIBBEAN CHOCOLATE CAKE

Siren Craft Brew and Cigar City Brewing, UK/USA

Type Imperial Stout **Strength** 7.4%

• It's fitting that Siren turned to Cigar City when crafting this imperial stout. The Tampa-based brewery is best known for its Hunahpu's Imperial Stout, which is brewed with cacao nibs, vanilla, cinnamon, and ancho and pasilla chillies, while this dessert-like imperial stout is made with cacao nibs, lactose, and fragrant cypress wood.

BLACK DAMNATION

De Struise Brouwers, Oostvleteren, Belgium

Type Imperial Stout **Strength** 13%

• Black Damnation began as a blend of two imperial stouts: Struise's Black Albert and De Molen's Hel & Verdoemenis (Hell & Damnation). Originally envisioned as a series of 12 beers, there are now over 25 variants, the most recent ('Black Nuts') being a blend aged in Ardbeg whisky barrels, adding intense oak and peat notes to the mountain of chocolate and coffee flavours.

TART OF DARKNESS

The Bruery Terreux, Anaheim, California, USA

Type Sour Stout **Strength** 7%

• In 2015, The Bruery begat The Bruery Terreux: a new brand devoted to farmhouse-style wild ales and oak-aged sours. Tart of Darkness – a stout aged in used, wild yeast-inoculated barrels – is one of the newer label's highlights. Seek out the variety that's aged with cherries and vanilla, an addition that complements the beer's baseline roasty malt, fruity yeast, and caramel oak character.

IMPERIAL STOUT LONDON 1856

The Kernel, London, UK
Type Imperial Stout **Strength** 9.5%

• London's The Kernel is perhaps better known for its pale ales, saisons and fruit sours, but miss out on its dark beers at your peril. This Imperial Brown Stout is based on an 1856 recipe from the archives of the former Barclay Perkin's brewery. Expect roasted malt character up front evoking memories of dark chocolate and espresso, leading to a drying, bitter finish.

BLACK MALTS AND BODY SALTS

To Øl, Copenhagen, Denmark
Type Black Imperial IPA **Strength** 9.9%

• Created by the nomadic To Øl – but produced in Belgium by De Proefbrouwerij – Black Malts and Body Salts is named in honour of the brewers whose sweat goes into the beers we love (sometimes literally). Described by To Øl as a Black Imperial IPA, though it could be categorised as a coffee beer or hoppy stout, this potent brew offers remarkable balance between its hops, dark malts, and coffee elements.

VERNAL MINTHE STOUT

SKA Brewing, Colorado USA
Type Stout **Strength** 5.8%

• One of the finest flavoured stouts in the world. Whole cacao nibs, vanilla, peppermint and spearmint go into this smooth, creamy and sweet stout. Its enormous, minty finish is the main attraction, instantly transporting you through time to your first taste of mint chocolate chip ice cream as a child. It's a sort of dessert/beer hybrid that converts so-called 'non-beer drinkers' instantly and permanently.

DOUBLE PERLE

Weird Beard Brewing Co, London, UK
Type Imperial Stout **Strength** 8.6%

• Double Perle, a 'double' version of Black Perle coffee milk stout, was first released in 2014 to celebrate 100 brews at Weird Beard Brewing Co. It packs a lot of coffee into its rich and roasty aroma, and its texture is almost velvety – think cold brew coffee with milk and a dash of chocolate syrup. The whisk(e)y barrel-aged versions are even more delicious.

BILLIONAIRE

Wild Beer Co, Shepton Mallet, UK
Type Imperial Stout **Strength** 10%

• One step up from the brewery's heralded Millionaire – a stout made with salted caramel and chocolate – the mighty Billionaire ups the ante with lactose, sea salt, caramelised miso paste, and tonka beans (as well as 10% alcohol content – sip slowly). Velvety on the palate, luxuriant Billionaire is perfect for dessert, though the miso supplies a dose of umami flavour that adds an extra level of profundity.

OLD PECULIER

Theakston, Masham, UK
Type Old Ale **Strength** 5.6%

• Whilst no longer considered strong by modern palates, the ale once known as 'Lunatic's Broth' still retains a certain reputation. If it's been a while since you last tried it or you haven't had the pleasure, give it a chance. There are treacly, toffee apple notes and moreish, soft fruit and nutty depths to this old-fashioned dark ale. Whilst not exactly a stout, as a roasty and fruity old ale it has a great deal in common with modern porter.

TEN FIDY STOUT

Oskar Blues Brewery, Colorado, USA
Type Stout **Strength** 10.5%

• Named for its prodigious strength, this outstanding stout shoots straight down the middle of flavours. Not too boozy, not too chocolatey, not too roasty, Ten FIDY still packs all of these flavours in abundance, but does so with zen-like balance. It actually seems to taste even better for it. What it lacks in extremism, it makes up for in clarity, balance, quality and freshness.

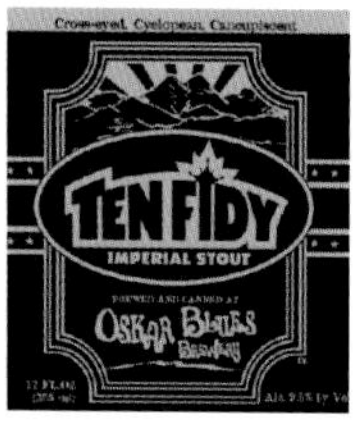

RAILWAY PORTER

Five Points Brewing Company, London UK
Type Porter **Strength** 4.8%

• Hackney-based Five Points are steadily building a range of really high-quality beers. Their Railway Porter is quite rich and astringent, sticky with treacly malt and roasted coffee beans that turn into chocolate syrup before exploding in waves of roasty bitterness and muscular hop notes of red berries and spice. A luxuriant, yet accessible, full-flavoured porter.

PUMKING

Southern Tier Brewing Company, USA
Type Pale Ale **Strength** 8.6%

• This bright amber, orange-tinted ale has lots of nutmeg and cinnamon in its potent, boozy aroma. Its warming flavour begins with cakey sweetness and pumpkin pie, before the spices take over, giving the palate a solid peppering as it gains heat in its sticky and dry finish.

CONQUEROR BLACK IPA

Windsor & Eton, Windsor UK
Type Black IPA **Strength** 5%

• This crisp and great-tasting black IPA delivers big smacks of flavour whilst staying eminently drinkable. Solid, toffee sweetness up front is sharpened by espresso bitterness, before it lets loose with fat, heavy wallops of refreshing, pithy hop fruit and floral notes. The 'Conqueror 1075' version delivers even bigger flavours at a markedly less sessionable 7.4% ABV.

BIGFOOT ALE

Sierra Nevada, California USA
Type Barleywine Style **Strength** 9.6%

• Bigfoot Ale is an old school beast of a beer, first released in 1983. The liberal application of whole hop cones give it a staggering bitterness level, balanced by lots of malt to create a big, bittersweet beer with resinous, woodland aromas, and sweet caramel, grapefruit and orange flavours.

SAMUEL ADAMS UTOPIAS

The Boston Brewery, Boston, USA
Type Strong Ale **Strength** 29%

• Utopias' rich, fruity sherry notes dominate on the first sip, but these quickly dissipate, revealing an intense and port-like character.

MARS

Atom, Hull, UK
Type Rye Wine **Strength** 11%

• The Hull-based brewery combines immense amounts of barley and rye malt with resinous, aromatic hops to produce a liquid with the same righteous pomp as the Gustav Holst composition of the same name.

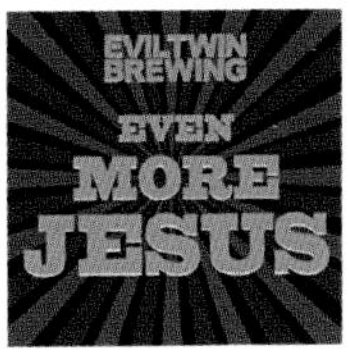

EVEN MORE JESUS

Evil Twin, Denmark
Type Stout **Strength** 12%

• This imperial stout from Evil Twin is about as big and angry as they get. It's heavy with boozy notes in the taste, balanced, only just, by even bigger flavours of darkest roast coffee and the darkest possible chocolate. Berries and brown sugar try to sweeten you up at first, but there's no escaping this beer's righteous anger.

JACOBITE ALE

Traquair House, Peeblesshire Scotland
Type Strong Ale **Strength** 8%

• This traditional Scottish beer is brewed at a Scottish stately home ruled by a Laird. It is brewed with coriander seed added into the boil, and is wonderfully fruity and sweet on the nose. There are perfumed, aniseed and liquorice flavours slightly reminiscent of a Belgian dubbel, but here built on a strong, Scotch ale body.

GALE'S PRIZE OLD ALE

Fuller's, London UK
Type Old Ale **Strength** 9%

• Gale's was revived by Fuller's a few years ago. Depending on its age, it can display Flanders-red-esque tart and sour notes, vinous fruits and a malt character. However, bottles in the best condition also have warming, sherry-like flavours, as well as chocolate, boiled sweets and stewed fruit notes.

DARK LORD

3 Floyds Brewing Co., Munster, Indiana, USA
Type Imperial Stout **Strength** 15%

• Dark Lord is an imperial stout that sees the cold light of day just once a year. This oubliette black, viscous liquid is rife with aromas of burnt sugar and soy sauce, with a similar umami quality on the palate, with a strong, cigar-like tobacco note in the finish.

TWEAK

Avery Brewing, Boulder, Colorado, USA
Type Imperial Stout **Strength** 16%

• This bourbon barrel-aged imperial stout uses maltose in addition to masses of malted barley and then adds coffee bringing out its roasted notes to mingle with flavours of molasses and alcohol.

HARVIESTOUN OLA DUBH 12

A viscous, whisky-barrel-aged beer that's a perfect treat at Christmas

Harviestoun use their excellent Old Engine Oil as the base for Engineer's Reserve and for each of the Old Dubh bottlings, which go from 12, 16, 18 and 30 to 40. The Ola Dubh series (which is Celtic for 'Black Oil') is aged in Highland Park whisky barrels.

The Ola Dubh numbers don't relate to the strength or age of the beer – they refer to the number of years the whisky has been aged. The 12, 16 and 18 are more commercially available, while grandmothers are often traded for the 30 and 40-year-old expressions.

Ola Dubh 12 pours a shade so black it must be what staring into the heart of a black hole looks like. A narrow, mocha-coloured head orbits briefly before it disappears under Ola Dubh's crushing gravity. In return, Ola Dubh gives out aromas of molasses, spiced rum, liquorice, toffee and umami yeast. It isn't regular molasses or normal liquorice – there's a very clear impression that all of these qualities have been distilled into their purest, smoothest essence, making for a very luxuriant aroma.

The viscous, velvety body carries waves of overlapping tastes; caramelised sugar and toffee sweetness lap over the tongue first, followed by vanilla and sarsaparilla. A midsection of whisky and wood sweeps in, the sublime Highland Park whisky notes sitting proudly at the core of the beer's taste, and then those whisky barrel flavours turn into charred oak and toasted malt. Finally, Ola Dubh bows out in a puff of smoke, like a magician finishing his act, leaving behind a faint afterimage of bittersweet dryness on the tongue.

the facts

Brewer Harviestoun
Origin Clackmannanshire, Scotland
Strength 6%
Type Vintage Strong Ale
Web www.harviestoun.com
Temperature 12-16°C

THE BEER TALKING

STUART CAIL

HARVIESTOUN CRAFT BREWERY

What made you want to become a brewer?
I did my best to remain a student for as long as possible. As some of my funding came from the Brewers' Society (as was) and of course the taxman, it only seemed fair to contribute back to them!

What's the inspiration behind Old Engine Oil Porter and Old Dubh 12?
The joy of being able to reinvent old recipes in the first instance and then turn them into something different and new in the second.

Which beer best demonstrates who you are as a brewery?
That would be Ola Dubh in terms of technicality, and Bitter & Twisted in terms of volume.

BOURBON COUNTY 2012

A super-strong stout aged in bourbon barrels. What's not to love?

Goose Island Bourbon County is a limited, annual release sold toward the end of each year. In case the name wasn't clue enough, Bourbon County is a stout aged in bourbon barrels. And boy what a stout! At 15% ABV it goes beyond beer and wine and starts to enter liqueur territory, so this is definitely something special, to be saved and savoured and popped open on special occasions. Goose Island claims it will age well for up to five years, so there's no rush to open one up.

When the time is right, though, Bourbon County fills the glass with a crude oil appearance. An ochre, ruddy head graces the top of this thick broth before swiftly disappearing. On the nose it's genuinely one of the nicest smelling beers out there – it's like Christmas fruit pudding caked in muscovado sugar. Instead of brandy it's been soaked in bourbon and glazed in honey. There's also a liquorice aroma that comes through strongly in the taste.

However, before the taste the first thing noticed with Bourbon County is the thick, chewy mouth feel – it isn't something you drink, rather something you nibble on. Then the liquorice returns, not as a hint or a background note, but as entire sticks of the stuff, soaked in bourbon, aged in wood and drizzled in cocoa. Hints of honeycomb, milk chocolate and spiced dark rum appear as outlines in the dark but, make no mistake, Bourbon County is deliciously heavy on brown sugar, bourbon and liquorice.

Surprisingly for a beer boasting 15% ABV, there's no obvious fire or burn – just a lingering, tingling spice on the tip of the tongue right at the finish. Even in a 330ml bottle, Bourbon County is perfect for sharing, particularly after a large dinner with friends but especially at 3am around the kitchen table with the brother-in-law after a night on the town.

the facts

Brewer Goose Island Beer Co.
Origin Chicago, Illinois, USA
Strength 15%
Type Stout
Web www.gooseisland.com
Temperature 12-16°C

THE BEER TALKING

BRETT PORTER

GOOSE ISLAND BEER COMPANY

What do you most enjoy about brewing?
I enjoy everything about brewing, but selecting hops and seeing the hop yards is the most enjoyable part of it for me. It rejuvenates and inspires me every year.

What's your favourite beer to drink after work?
My favourite drink after work at home is Leffe Blonde. I love many beers, but I never tire of Leffe. I sometimes tell people Leffe is my favourite beer to lean on a rake with, while my wife does all the real work in our garden.

Which beers do you wish you had made?
Duchesse de Bourgogne from Brewery Verhaeghe and Wadworth's Farmers Glory.

TRIPEL B
Funkwerks
SAISON D'BRETT
SPECIALE
DE GARDE
SAISON DUPONT
CHIMAY
GRANDE RÉSERVE ALE
Matilda
ATHENA
DNR
SAVE THE WORLD
Bitter
Belgian Golden Ale
STOUT
REAL ALE BREWING CO
Sisyphus
SISYPHUS
HARVEST ALE
BAPTIST
IMPERIAL STOUT
GOSE
WILD SOUR
Founders
Green Zebra
G&T GOSE